Fishing Florida's Flats

WILD FLORIDA

UNIVERSITY PRESS OF FLORIDA

Florida A&M University, Tallahassee
Florida Atlantic University, Boca Raton
Florida Gulf Coast University, Ft. Myers
Florida International University, Miami
Florida State University, Tallahassee
New College of Florida, Sarasota
University of Central Florida, Orlando
University of Florida, Gainesville
University of North Florida, Jacksonville
University of South Florida, Tampa
University of West Florida, Pensacola

University Press of Florida
Gainesville · Tallahassee · Tampa · Boca Raton · Pensacola
Orlando · Miami · Jacksonville · Ft. Myers · Sarasota

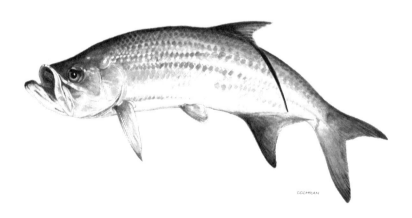

Illustrations by Vaughn Cochran

Fishing Florida's Flats

A Guide to Bonefish, Tarpon, Permit, and Much More

Jan S. Maizler

Foreword by M. Timothy O'Keefe

With contributions by Tim Borski, Vaughn Cochran,
Captain Butch Constable, Captain Jon Cooper,
Captain Bill Curtis, Pat Ford, Scott S. Heywood,
Captain John Kumiski, Captain Mike Locklear, Captain Greg Poland,
Captain Tom Rowland, and Captain Robert "RT" Trosset

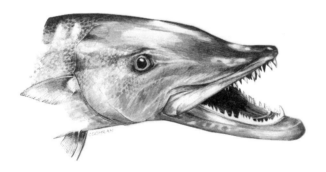

Illustrations by Vaughn Cochran

WILD FLORIDA

Edited by M. Timothy O'Keefe

Books in this series are written for the many people who visit and/or move to Florida to participate in our remarkable outdoors, an environment rich in birds, animals, and activities, many exclusive to this state. Books in the series offer readers a variety of formats: natural history guides, historical outdoor guides, guides to some of Florida's most popular pastimes and activities, and memoirs of outdoors folk and their unique lifestyles.

30 Eco-trips in Florida: The Best Nature Excursions and How to Reduce Your Impact on the Environment, by Holly Ambrose (2005)

A Hiker's Guide to the Sunshine State, by Sandra Friend (2005)

Fishing Florida's Flats: A Guide to Bonefish, Tarpon, Permit, and Much More, by Jan S. Maizler (2007)

50 Great Walks in Florida, by Lucy Beebe Tobias (2007)

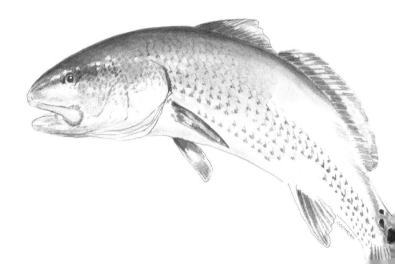

12 11 10 09 08 07   6 5 4 3 2 1

Library of Congress Cataloging-in-Publication Data
A record of cataloging-in-publication data is available from
the Library of Congress.

ISBN 978-0-8130-3145-3

Cover. Top: Captain Bob Trosset poles his anglers over the beautiful
waters of the Florida Keys. Photo by Pat Ford. *Bottom, left to right*:
Jumped One and *Permit*. Paintings by Vaughn Cochran.

The University Press of Florida is the scholarly publishing agency
for the State University System of Florida, comprising Florida
A&M University, Florida Atlantic University, Florida Gulf Coast
University, Florida International University, Florida State University,
New College of Florida, University of Central Florida, University of
Florida, University of North Florida, University of South Florida,
and University of West Florida.

University Press of Florida
15 Northwest 15th Street
Gainesville, FL 32611-2079
http://www.upf.com

To Nathan Maizler, whose courage and vision
taught me that life is about experience, not acquisition.

Illustration by Vaughn Cochran

Contents

Foreword

The University Press of Florida celebrates the essential natural qualities of Florida, its environment, its creatures, and its people through the broad-ranging series *Wild Florida*. *Fishing Florida's Flats*, by veteran angler and former International Game Fish Association record-holder Jan Maizler, illustrates the wide-ranging approach to UPF's commitment to exploring, appreciating, and protecting our wild Florida.

With Florida ranked as one of the most populous states and hundreds of thousands more moving here every year, it seems impossible that truly wild places can remain anywhere in such a densely inhabited region.

Yet in spite of the tremendous influx of people wanting to enjoy the Sunshine State's warm climate and active outdoors lifestyle, significant sections of the original, natural Florida do still endure.

In fact the amount of land and shoreline Florida has set aside for preservation surprises many people, especially first-time visitors and newly arrived residents. As this is written, Florida terrain is protected by three national forests, 11 national parks, 157 state parks, and 28 national wildlife refuges. In addition, individual counties have designated their own protected public lands, providing for pristine rivers and sheltered coastline.

Yes, there is quite a lot of Florida that hasn't been paved over or disturbed by development, and it never will be.

Although expensive offshore sportfishing boats with their flying bridges and outriggers tend to symbolize Florida fishing to visitors and newcomers, many serious local anglers never fish the deeper waters. They've learned the most appealing angling action is on or beside the shallow flats bordering the state's shoreline.

In his 45 years of angling, Jan Maizler not only has caught but has released over 2,000 bonefish, and he once held the IGFA record for bonefish on two-pound test line and permit on four-pound test.

However, every serious angler like Jan tends to have his favorite quarry, and for Jan it's definitely the bonefish in the waters of Biscayne Bay.

Recognizing that no one angler can know it all, Jan asked eight of Florida's top professional flats guides to share their secrets of how-to, when-to, and where-to. Each guide is a specialist of a different game fish species in separate parts of the state. The overall result is that no other book has ever come close to providing such complete, in-depth flats fishing information by the top guides, who must prove daily they can please demanding clients with a good, satisfying day of angling.

Fishing Florida's Flats is a book serious fishermen will find themselves referring to frequently because there is far more information than can be digested in one or two sittings. This is the most thorough body of work ever assembled about Florida flats game fishing, and all of it is provided by the top experts.

Still, professional guides are an individualistic breed with their own particular style of doing things. It is a testament to Jan's reputation as a fishing flats expert that they were willing to contribute to this book. Moreover, the guides moderated some of their individualism and conformed to Jan's master format, which makes their material consistently presented and easily resourced throughout the book.

Their willingness illustrates just how special *Fishing Florida's Flats* is and why it deserves to become a classic reference. The bulk of this knowledge has never been presented before with such impeccable authority.

M. Timothy O'Keefe
Series Editor

Preface

This book is a studious celebration of Florida's flats fish and the flats themselves. It is also a chronicle and tribute to the wonderful Florida fishing guides who have made flats fishing into such an explosively popular fishing specialty. *Fishing Florida's Flats* is designed as a handbook to tweak open the doors of a shallow water paradise for anglers who do, or will, fish the shallows of the Sunshine State. I want to express my thanks and gratitude to all the contributors to this book. They are all experts whose excellent written advice, instruction, and inspired images will throw those doors open even wider.

Fishing Florida's Flats is designed for people who want to take up the sport of flats fishing. To make the most of the experience, all that's needed is the most basic knowledge of light tackle fishing—in either fresh or salt water. Although many readers may be first-timers to the flats of Florida, more experienced anglers will find plenty of informative material by the numerous experts that will be sure to improve anyone's angling approaches and techniques on our flats.

My objective is to speak to the broadest possible base of reader-anglers. This certainly includes the newest generation of shallow water anglers—our youth. It has been gratifying to gather so much collective knowledge, and I hope it will inspire new adventurers awaiting a quest where hunting, fishing, and reverence blend under a bright, bold, Florida sun.

The Shallow Water Quest

I have a fair number of friends who are perennial world travelers and wanderers. Though I travel a great deal, I am basically a steadfast Floridian with fifty-eight years of sand in my shoes. Recently, I had a reunion with one such globetrotting chum—his name is Brad. Regardless of the frequency of our contacts, our discussions have, in my estimation, been thorough and thoughtful.

The setting for our get-together this time was a delightful restaurant in Key Largo overlooking a large saltwater lake that connects to vast Florida Bay. We timed our reservation to coincide with the sunset. It turned out that we were blessed with just the right amount of horizon clouds that, mixed with the dropping sun, gave us a sky show highlighted in yellow, orange, salmon, and blue. At one moment, the sun peeked through the multicolored display and threw a molten golden line across the water right to our table. We raised our glasses to toast the sun and then we talked on.

The direction and flow of our conversation was a bit like the tide—something with a discernible direction but also featuring novel meanders and rivulets. As the fading half-sun eased below the water's horizon line and the sky transitioned to a deeper blue, we discussed our respective choices in saltwater angling—each of which had become a lifelong pursuit.

Brad's passion for fishing took him far past my beloved shallows all the way out to the Gulf Stream. Like Hemingway, he would troll across Florida's azure depths in vessels much larger than mine in the hopes of hooking sailfish, marlin, dolphin, and tuna. He loved the idea that he was never quite sure what gamester would rise up to find and crash his baits. Brad's joy has been envelopment in the mysteries of how he could get fish to come to him.

In contrast, my joy has been solving this mystery by going to the fish instead. Since I was a teenager, my method of pursuit has been and still is a sixteen-foot shallow draft skiff that is poled around hunting grounds often no deeper than a foot.

After years of Brad's trolling and my poling, we have both been left tanned by the sun and burnished by the wind.

And with the last tiny arc of sun dropping into the Florida Bay horizon and the sky now graduating upward from dark blue to indigo with diamond stars, Brad and I agreed that we were both on the angler's quest. We were driven by the adventure that fishing in Florida's waters so often creates. Our abilities were derived from years of training and experience, kept strong by a solid perseverance that would not allow hardship or disappointment to keep us from attaining our grail.

I explained to Brad the passionate anticipation of flats anglers that causes the night before the trip to be so full of fishy dreams, restless tossing about, and alarm clock glances. Brad shared the same sweaty night-before experience when someone gave him the coordinates of a new offshore seamount that quite possibly teemed with tuna and marlin.

As our meeting ended and we returned to our individual lives and quests, we emerged with a strong connection between us and a keen realization that the angling quest comes in many forms.

Florida's Flats Fishing Cornucopia

Florida is a cornucopia for flats anglers. No other state or country in the world has the unique combination of so many diverse shallow water species that attain such world-record sizes. Florida's flats have given up trophy catches of bonefish, tarpon, permit, redfish, and sharks. When you add in the large barracuda, seatrout, and snook, it is an inescapable conclusion that Florida is thoroughly unique and unmatched on the planet. In the Florida Keys, an annual tournament targets redfish and bonefish on the flats, and Florida is the only place such a combo can be achieved. Some faraway destinations have large numbers of unpressured flats fish, but in my estimation, they do not have the absolute diversity of species or sizes of individuals. As a bonus, Florida also has what I call the "fun fish" of the flats. The deeper flats off Tampa feature large cruising cobia at certain times of year. On the beach flats off Cape Sable and south of Naples, you can catch tailing pompano if the tides are right. Amidst certain grassflat areas in Florida Bay, hard-pulling jacks and leaping ladyfish are an ongoing possibility.

Flats Hot Spots

This book directs you to flats fish hot spots throughout the state of Florida. If you are hunting for trophy or world-record-sized flats fish in Florida, these are the shallow water areas in which you may want to start. Be sure to check the chapters on weather and on each individual species, so as to know the best times to go.

Today's Technology

Flats anglers in this age of technology—with electronic and Internet tools—have never been so well equipped in their quest. Satellites orbiting the earth provide us with much more help than the early Florida flats fishermen had in their explorations.

For instance, you are now able to purchase a remarkably small and compact electronic unit that features a Global Positioning System and Chartplotter for your skiff console. Put in the simplest terms, this device uses an integrated system of satellites and map software to tell you where you are on the planet, where you have been before (via stored memory), and where your course will take you. These units also come in handheld models that can be used by wading anglers. Many of the devices are waterproof.

Although the flats are shallow waters into which you can see, having a device to help you find and remember a new hot spot offers vast advantages on the flats. It obviates the need to take visual shoreline ranges to determine your position, and on some of Florida's vast flats, this crude method is not viable anyway. The handheld units are so powerful that charter boat customers are banned from bringing them onboard vessels that rely on offshore "honeyhole" reefs and wrecks for their livelihood.

Another potent search-explore-and-discover tool is on the Internet. It is a program called Google Earth—A 3D Interface to the Planet. The URL or address for this Web site is http://earth.google.com. In the words of the site itself, Google Earth "puts a planet's worth of imagery and other geographic information right on your desktop." The satellite and aircraft images in Google Earth have been updated on a rolling basis over the last three years. Your computer must have specific capabilities to utilize this application.

Another Internet tool that will help your discovery quest is Google Local (http://maps.google.com). You can retrieve map, satellite, and hybrid images of our planet that you can zoom in on, back out of, or drag with your mouse. I find the satellite maps the simplest and most powerful exploratory tools. Although the mosaic of patched images covers the planet, not all areas can be viewed at the highest resolution. Fortunately, the flats of Florida have zoomable images that offer tremendous detail. Using this program, you can explore all of coastal Florida and predict potentially fruitful flats. I believe this program is an absolute necessity—if you try it, you will too.

Seekers and Guides

Although your quest will not take you to the summit of the icy heights of Mount Everest, like Edmund Hilary and his Sherpa, Tenzing Norgay, their effectiveness as a team comprising both seekers and a local expert parallels the best of flats fishing in several ways. Famed treasure hunter Mel Fisher also utilized a team of multiple talents, fueled by the encouraging words, "today's the day."

The shallow water quest is the heart and spirit of flats fishing, and I believe Florida's guides and captains play a crucial role in the pursuit of and triumph over the particular flats species you seek. These fine people provide the quickest way to learn, thrive, and grow in your flats fishing quests. They also lead the way to new locales, adventures, and experiences in a way that is irreplaceable. Some of Florida's best flats fishing guides have contributed to this book in a generous gesture to help you on your way. Without even stepping into their boats, your journey has begun!

History and Origins of Florida Flats Fishing

Long Key and Islamorada are starting points for flats fishing in the Florida Keys.

The initial popularization of flats fishing involved the angling pursuits of writer Zane Grey at the Long Key Fishing Club. My research indicates that although his fishing at the club popularized the area, most of his initial angling efforts focused on kingfish and sailfish offshore and tarpon inshore. His obsession with the bonefish soon followed as he observed other club anglers going about some mysterious business.

His accounts of the bonefish in *Tales of Fishes* in 1919 give it a mythical status. His rare work in 1922, "The Bonefish Brigade," is a tribute to this fish and a story of his chums at the Long Key Fishing Club. The piece can be found at www.duckkeyonline.com/duck_key_history/text_of_bonefish_brigade.htm.

Grey was a dentist-turned-cowboy, then a writer and angler. The flats he fished were around Long Key and Duck Key. When permit and bonefish were his targets, Zane Grey used eighteen-pound test on conventional gear rigged with a sinker and a hook baited with half of a fresh blue crab. He often still-fished from an anchored canoe or skiff on the flats. At times, he would cast from the beach and wait for the rising tide to bring a fish to the scent of his bait. Flats fishing in the teens of the century was not a sight-and-cast fishery, and eighteen-pound test was considered light tackle.

Long Key was originally known as Viper Key, then Long Island, eventually to be named Long Key. The Long Key Fishing Club was formed in 1917 with Zane Grey as its president. The Hurricane of 1935 put an end to the club—its only remnants are in photos, books, and memory.

Time and tide rolled on. A natural catastrophe ended the club, but man-made catastrophes occurred as well, like the Great Depression and World War II. How you react to catastrophe—whether natural or man-made—may determine the course of your life. In those live-or-die, good and bad times, you could crumble, struggle, or even triumph. But better yet, you could simply fish—an idea only a natural-born angler can understand.

During those globally troubled times, the nucleus of flats fishing efforts drifted up the Keys to Islamorada, where a shift from light conventional tackle to fly tackle took place.

Although sight-and-cast fishing from a poled boat on the flats was becoming increasingly popular throughout the Keys, the Islamorada area was the epicenter of those efforts. In 1939, Captain Bill Smith of Islamorada became the first angler who deliberately caught a cruising bonefish on fly tackle. After the war, in the summer of 1947, Joe Brooks—guided by Captain Jimmie Albright—made his mark by being the first angler credited with taking the first tailing bonefish on fly tackle. He reputedly caught another tailing bonefish on the same trip. These two anglers popularized bonefishing on the flats, but the exponential development of fishing Florida's flats for all the marine species that lived on or visited the shallows was given a jet-assisted takeoff by the countless guides and anglers who came rushing in.

Flats fishing history was also being made north of Islamorada in Miami. In 1948, a young man from Oklahoma by the name of Bill Curtis began fishing the crystal shallows of Biscayne Bay within the shadows of the downtown Miami skyline. He quickly learned that its waters were teeming with bonefish, tarpon, and permit. He found large schools of bonefish five minutes from the Crandon marina. He often spent the entire day catching bonefish within sight of the boat ramp.

Compared to the preceding two decades, the 1950s were years of plenty—first with a car in the garage and then with a television in the

The spinning reel revolutionized flats fishing. Photo by Bass Pro Shops.

living room. At home, you could now see the news instead of merely hearing it. But two developments affected the future of flats fishing forever. The first was the invention and mass production of spinning tackle. This made many more types of light tackle fishing possible on the flats and in all salt waters. The simplicity of spinning attracted more anglers to Florida's shallows. It also made the challenges of ultralight lines of two- and four-pound test reachable in a way that fly tackle simply could not.

The second development was twofold. In the late 1950s, Bill Curtis became the first professional fishing guide to offer poled charters on the flats of Biscayne Bay. No longer did you need to drive to the Keys to obtain the services of a flats fishing guide—you could fly to Miami, and while your family romped on the sands of a growing Miami Beach, you could meet your guide minutes from downtown and head to the adventures of nearby flats. This formula was a winner, and from those times to the present, Bill Curtis's tutelage and sponsorship of countless guides has filled Florida's flats from Miami to Islamorada with some of its finest captains.

Bill made flats fishing history in another way. On one particularly foul-weather day when traditional spotting on the flats was impossible, Bill developed a technique of chumming over white spots that proved to be an instant success. From that point on, chumming became a tool for countless flats guides and anglers, who added a fishing method that was exciting, productive, and one they could use when they had to or simply wanted to do so.

In the ensuing forty or fifty years, shallow saltwater sight fishing has evolved into a fishing specialty that is practiced all over the world. Florida can be proud of having given birth to modern flats fishing.

Wading Florida's Flats

If you really want to get the number of any particular Florida flat, you'd do best to let "your feet do the walking through the shallow places." This reinvention of that popular old slogan connotes that wading is not just an effective flats fishing strategy—it's also one of the best possible ways of learning the subtleties of a flat that cannot be realized while poling from a floating platform.

Your first step—in both senses of the word—is to be sure that the flat is "wadable." Florida has three basic types of flats: mud-marl flats, sandflats, and rubble or reef flats. Seagrass may be present on top—especially in the first two types—and may visually obscure the bottom. Mudflats and reef flats tend to be relatively hazardous for wading.

Mudflats can collapse like quicksand. These soft flats generally form inland in lagoons and bays. If you suspect the bottom is soft, probe it with your pushpole first. If you are already wading and the bottom begins to give way, do not panic. Simply turn around and leave in the direction from which you came. Many wading anglers tend to think that the only hazardous bottoms are the overly soft variety. This limited view can be a big mistake.

Reef flats, or rubble flats, front the open ocean. They can be quite dangerous for wading because the configuration of the flats floor can trip you or, worse yet, trap your foot in a rocky pocket. I saw such an incident once off the Ragged Keys in southern Biscayne Bay. I watched two anglers about a hundred yards to my north get out of their skiff to begin wading. It was obvious from their position that they were attempting to put the sneak on some permit close to a rock pile in extremely calm conditions. Despite my waving them off, they proceeded forward. Within a minute both anglers had stumbled, and the next minute, one of them tripped face first into the water. If you want to wade a reef flat, check it out first by snorkeling the area on a midday high tide.

Generally, the safest flats are sandflats. Although they are the most stable type of flat for wading on, even sandflats necessitate caution because the bottom is often contoured into valleys and hills. Long wades over these bottoms can become treks that can be tiring if you are not physically fit. If you have any limiting condition, it is essential to have a definite idea of how long your wade will be, even if it is over good bottom. If your doctor has determined that you are simply out of shape, speak with him or her about commencing some type of graduated cardiovascular training program at the local gym. Adjustable treadmills, stair climbers, ellipticals, and erect and recumbent bikes are all good equipment to help potential waders get in shape. Wading involves a strong, viable heart-lung-leg connection.

Wading at low tide can reveal important flats fish highways. Photo by Scott Heywood/Angling Destinations.

Find a contour on the flats and you're likely to hook up. Photo by Scott Heywood/ Angling Destinations.

If you have access to a skiff or kayak, you can use the vessel to explore a new flat that you intend to wade. Simply pole or paddle the area on a high tide and, from the luxury and safety of a floating platform, probe the bottom frequently for firmness. Use the bottom or foot of your pushpole as your bottom probe because it is the end that more accurately represents your wading anatomy.

It is not wise to base your wading safety on casual talk or advice, even if it comes from a tackle shop. Instead, find a fishing friend and explore the area together. Both of you should carry some type of hand probe: an old bridge stick from a pool table or pool hall can be quite good. I take the position that it is generally wiser to use the buddy system on first-time wading explorations. Alternatively, you can hire a local fishing guide who specializes in wade trips.

Laws and guidelines specify life jackets aboard vessels. As a wader, you are now a "man overboard"—it is only a few short steps from the shin-deep flat into the six-foot channel alongside you. The advantages of a life jacket to waders are numerous, and the disadvantages are nonexistent. The newest models of life jackets are sleek, crisp, and unencumbering.

The best conditions for familiarizing yourself with a flat to be waded or poled are when the overhead lighting is the best for seeing the bottom. Low tide explorations reveal the most features, but your initial approach should occur when conditions are safe and groundings are minimized. Extra caution must be exercised on reef flats to avoid harm to people, vessels, and the reef itself. For most flats investigations, a midday low tide is desirable, but pay attention to whether a full or new moon yields unusually low tides and thus creates risks.

As you explore, be sure to take along a camera, notepad, and waterproof pen. You can store these items in a lip-sealed clear plastic container or bag. Document what you see as frequently as possible by making notes and sketches or taking photos. In the future, you can refer to your records time and again.

Watching and Wading

The major strategic value of wading for flats fish is stealth. Wading creates a descent into the water column, which gives an angler a much lower profile than a skiff. A lower profile helps avoid spooking the fish; however, flats fish spook just as often from movement, so move extremely slowly and be ready to freeze and squat to minimize the possibility of the fish seeing you as a threatening life form.

Waders should always be aware that they have a seesaw, inverse relationship to flats fish. When the fish start breaking the surface with their tail fins or dorsal fins as they tail or cruise, you should drop to the water to reduce your profile. As the waters deepen and you have to look through the water to spot cruising bonefish and redfish, or snook laid up in a pothole, you can extend yourself to your tallest height to maximize your spotting capabilities.

As you begin wading, transform yourself into a total flats scanning device. Your eyes are especially well suited to see potholes, channel drop-offs, grass clumps, and small rock piles. All of these structures may hold shallow water game fish on both low and high tides. In this hunting division of labor, the soles of your feet will do their job in detecting the subtle bottom contours and variations that your eyes are unable to see. With training, your foot soles will be excellent sensors, even when they are enclosed in the most protective footgear.

Possibly the most important features your feet may detect are bottom furrows or ruts, some of which may actually run across the flat into deeper channels or low tide holding basins. These bottom features can be extremely important in determining what fish will use as entry and exit minihighways for that particular flat. Interestingly, the fish may even follow these contours during the higher phases of the tide.

Wading Gear

When wading the flats, you'll be wearing many items that you would otherwise have stored in a boat or tackle bag. These include:

- Chest pack or fanny pack
- Fishing cap with long peak with dark underside
- Flies
- Hemostat or pliers
- Hooks and hook file
- Leader material
- Leatherman tool or knife
- Lighter
- Line cleaner and line nipper
- Lures
- Medicine—emergency and regular
- Polarized brown sunglasses with side shields
- Rain jacket
- Reel lube
- Split shot
- Sunscreen
- Water bottles

As far as apparel goes, I believe Florida's weather demands the respect and preparation that the name Sunshine State implies. It is always best to wear the popular back-vented long-sleeved shirts that feature big breast pockets with holes for paying out leader material. Because Florida's waters are so rich in multitudes of sea life—some species of which bite or sting—a matching pair of long wading pants is recommended. Be sure the colors of your shirt and pants are earth colors. After years of research with different types of footgear, I believe there is nothing better than plain white socks topped off with flats booties or over-ankle wading shoes. These are generally made of neoprene with hard rubber bottoms, corrosion-proof zippers, and Velcro closure straps on top to keep out the water. I usually tuck my pants into my wading shoes before tightening them up. This particular footgear arrangement is peerless in coping with all three flats bottom types and prevents cutting, punctures, loading with sand, or harming your skin.

Wading Techniques

If you have ever observed wading birds on the flats, I'm sure you appreciated their slow, methodical, yet incredibly effective hunting techniques. Consider them your mentors and emulate them as much as you are able. Always be aware that fast wading with your thick human legs will give off a pressure wave that flats fish will detect, so slow down and try to blend in with the flat.

Several factors will affect your wading and walking style. A calm day of flat water will force you to tighten your wading style latitude because the fish hear so much better than on the more forgiving windy days. When wading, move with a slight shuffling motion to push stingrays and crabs away from your path. A regular stepping motion will land your feet directly over these creatures and risks injury. In addition, regular stepping on a flat is noisy and obtrusive. The other method of wading is one I call the "point and step" and is very effective in achieving a swifter method of wading over hard sand bottom after brisk fish like permit. The point and step involves raising your feet alternately out of the water and creating a very quiet walk by having only the points of your feet enter the water and flexing each foot into a landing position just before it touches the bottom.

Wade Fishing Strategies

When wading, your fishing strategy should be to spot a flats fish before it spots you, and then make your presentation. Look for related life forms like rays, sharks, crabs, egg casings, and worm holes that tell you the flat is alive and well. Pay particular attention to structures that will likely hold fish at some point in the tidal cycle.

On low tides, always give potholes a visual check for holdout fish like bonefish and redfish. On deeper flats or higher tides where spotting fish is more difficult, it is always a wise practice to fan cast the entire pothole from top to bottom for hide-and-pounce predators like snook and seatrout. Potholes are easily spotted because of their darker color and ovoid shapes, which stand out against the surrounding lighter flats bottom.

Small channels and cuts that lead into and out of a flat are wonderful places to station yourself to ambush traveling flats fish. These tiny fish highways are generally most evident on sand flats. Try to have the sun at your back so that you can see the fish optimally. As you stand and wait, periodically stretch and roll your spine and move your legs up and down to cut down on the muscle discomfort that sometimes accompanies long vigils in a stationary position. Staking out cuts when wading can result in some very productive bonefishing.

Two types of solid structures on the flats demand attention. The first type are structures like blown-down trees, which serve primarily as hiding places for ambush feeders like snook. The second type are structures like oyster bars and rock piles, which serve as shallow water cafeterias full of edible life-forms that live around or within the structure itself. Redfish and permit are notorious for patrolling the latter type of structure for crabs and other hard-shelled organisms. Black sea urchin remains filled the stomach of my ex-world-record permit (23 pounds, 15 ounces, on four-pound test). The fact that you discovered these hot spots on the low tide enables you to locate them during a rising tide as more fish swim into the structure for a protein meal.

Some Wading Tackle Considerations

As a wader, you have descended into the water when you hook a flats fish, so it stands to reason that more line will be in the water than if you were on top of a bonefish skiff (all other things being equal). More line in the water means more of a chance for cutoffs, pulled hooks from grassed-up line bellies, and popped ultralight tippets from fly line bellies. The best way to compensate for this and to get more line out of the water is to utilize the longest rods possible. When I switched from a standard seven-foot spinning rod to a nine-and-a-half-foot model many years ago, my cutoff rates dropped dramatically. If you love plug casting tackle the way I do, consider changing to a wading rod at least six-and-a-half-feet long. Fly rods are less of a concern because of their standard nine-foot length. Maximizing line out of the water during hookup and battle when you wade is always a good practice, and it is even more important on reef flats and mudflats with tall grass forests.

It is not always possible for waders to run after a hooked fish. Thus it is essential for your reel to have a huge line capacity, so that you won't get spooled. Sandy bottoms are perfectly adapted to monofilament lines. Use different lines when you wade over different bottoms. Soft monofilament is well adapted to smooth, sandy bottoms. When the flats bottom is composed of reef or deep grass, switch over to abrasion-resistant microbraid lines like PowerPro.

Flats Hot Spots: Wading for Bonefish

Long Key State Recreation Area is located at Mile Marker 67.5 on the Overseas Highway in the Florida Keys. This Atlantic-side destination has some of the world's most easily accessed flats in which you can wade for bonefish. On the high tide, the fish swim right against the campground beach. At low tide, they tail up a bit farther offshore. This delightful spot has created lifetime memories by providing a trophy catch for camping families new to bonefishing. All it takes to land a trophy catch is a good eight-pound spinning outfit, a 1/0 hook, and a live shrimp.

This wader is releasing his bonefish properly. Photo by Scott Heywood/Angling Destinations.

This snook was swimming in six inches of water when it was hooked. Photo by Art Blank.

Flats Hot Spots: Wading for Snook

Some of Florida's most accessible and productive fisheries for snook are the beach flats of southwest Florida from the beaches of Marco Island up to Captiva Island. The spring and summer months in Florida are characterized by calming seas in the presence of rising air and water temperatures. Generally, the first days of May bring the snook out of the bays into the passes for spawning. These snook congregations splinter off and fan out along the Gulf beaches to feed and spawn in smaller groups. You can access the southwest Florida beach flats by parking in one of the many nearby parking lots and walking over the beach path right to the surf's edge.

A similar spawning aggregation occurs on Florida's Atlantic side from Stuart to Miami; however, the snook are less numerous and far less visible on the rapid drop-offs of the Atlantic beaches, which feature no beach flats.

During calm weather, try wading for snook in the Bowman's Beach area on Sanibel Island. Another outstanding spot is about a half mile west of the West Wind Inn on the same island. When conditions were right, I've released over thirty snook a day fishing these two hot spots.

Tactics and Techniques for Gulf Coast Beach Flat Snooking

The first thing to realize is that you will be fishing for snook in less than a foot of water as they swim parallel to the beach, often only a foot from the sand. This type of wade fishing employs exactly the same "see-the-fish-first and cast" methods that you utilize in bonefishing. It is important to have some level of sunlight to help you see into the water to keep your stealth advantage. The best times for the light are from 8:00 a.m. to 4:00 p.m. Of course, you can blind-cast the area outside these times, but you'll be spooking many fish and you will lose the "bonefish" feel.

The basic rule with this fishery is that you must be as unobtrusive and invisible as possible. These snook are foraging for minnows and crabs in waters as shallow as six inches. I recently caught a six-pound fish working the "wash" with its back out of the water. Beach flat snook are on high alert as the hunter and the hunted. They are extremely aware of any overhead or peripheral movement and will spook for deeper water if they are the least bit suspicious. Snook have been programmed from the fry stage to flee from large moving shapes—once the predator was a sea bird; now it is you.

In the morning the rising eastern sun is at your back, so the risk of your silhouette and shadow spooking out the beach flat snook is high. Early in the day, it is best to begin your stalking a good distance from the water's edge. As with any flats fishing, you should wear a long-billed cap with a dark underside and glare-blocking polarized sunglasses. Slowly begin your walk, and if you spot a beach flat snook headed your way, very slowly crouch with subtle movement. The fish generally move parallel to the water's edge, so "feather" a cast a good five feet in front of the fish. If you cast too close, you will spook it out. Casting a little too far away is properly cautious, as the fish will continue "tracking" on a straight path. Just wait until the fish is a few feet away before you start an enticing retrieve by having your tiny bucktail kick up a few puffs of sand. Be sure to feather your lure before it lands to avoid a frightening plop. These fish were not designed to expect their food to come crashing from the sky. In this fishery in which summertime generally brings glassy calm conditions to the Gulf beach flats, sudden disturbing noises will send the snook fleeing for deeper water.

You will be pleased to know that these Florida beach flat snook cruise the area all day long. Like bonefish, the snook have learned to be sensitive to differing water heights and sand flat contours in their predatory search for food. Seeing a fifteen-pound snook working the shallows with its dorsal and tail fins exposed is sure to excite any Florida flats fisherman.

As the sun arcs into the west with the afternoon's unfolding, you'll again want the sun at your back for effectively spotting these fish. Making your approach with the sun at your back means going into the water to about twenty-five to thirty feet offshore of the water's edge and looking toward the beach from your "outside" vantage point. Generally, fish will be coming from one direction. In the Marco to Naples Beach area, I have seen more beach flat snook heading in a northerly direction. In the mornings, make your casts from the sand to the water, and in the afternoons, cast from the water toward the sand.

Whatever your position, do not make any sudden moves or any obvious overhead casts—this spooks beach flat snook. A modified side-arm cast will be less likely to be seen by your quarry. I am convinced that an overhead cast is generally the most accurate and easily learned approach. Good side-arm casting takes a great deal of practice.

On a clean open beach flat, a spinning outfit of true saltwater ability spooled with six-pound clear monofilament line is fine. The terminal end should feature a doubled line knotted to a thirty-pound fluorocarbon leader of twenty inches, and armed with a ⅛-ounce flathead white bucktail.

It is now fairly common to see beach flat pompano cruising the shallows off south-west Florida. This one grabbed a jig in one foot of water. Photo by Art Blank.

Even if these snook behave like bonefish, the snook in them reas-serts itself if they encounter any structure on the beach flat. Their true nature as hide-and-lunge ambush feeders is best served in and around rocks or blown-down trees where they can hide and pounce on the passing crabs and minnows in barely a foot of water. I carry a five-foot, twelve-pound plug rod stuffed into my waistband behind me for such occasions. It is rigged similarly to the spinner but can wrestle out beach flat snook that I encounter grouped near rocks or trees.

Fly tackle is capable of the most delicate presentations and soft landings. An eight-weight outfit works quite well and should be "finished" with a thirty-pound fluorocarbon bite tippet armed with a minnow-sized fly, like a Clouser-type that features some flash. The two problems that fly tackle brings to beach flat fishing for snook are the spooking that can occur from false casts and having your fly line land on the fish. When you use fly tackle, be cautious not to spook snook with your fly line. Feel confident of a quiet landing with even a fair cast. With spinning, the opposite is generally true—your line is less obvious to the fish, but the landing of your lure becomes the object of your caution.

Beach flat snook are most comfortable on the rising tide. Ideal conditions are a rising tide, clear water, mild breeze, overhead light, baitfish aggregations, and varied water-edge bottom contours. I have often seen snook working the beach flat with their backs out of the water on the early rising tide. The fish have obviously been there long enough to know that the wavelets of the rising tide will keep them wet and increasingly submerged.

In recent years I have seen pompano periodically flit into the surf line and tail up on tiny crabs. I have also cast to and caught sighted redfish. One thing is certain: this wader's paradise opens up to us every year when the warming waters of late spring come to the southwest Florida coast.

4

Flats Vessels

Consider your flats fishing situations as tiers of necessity. The first tier is pure, unassisted wading. In some situations in Florida, wading and fishing a flat is nicely accomplished on foot-power alone. Such examples of easy wades are bonefishing the ocean shoreline of Long Key State Park, wading the beaches of Marco Island, or casting certain grassflats of the Indian River for trout or snook. When you are unable to wade the rich and varied flats of Florida, you can utilize successive tiers of necessity, which include kayaks, flats boats, and bay boats.

The Kayak

Kayaks fill a much-needed niche in flats fishing situations and may be considered the second tier of necessity. If the distance from your starting point to your flat and back again is easily done by paddling (and you cannot wade to this area), your best choice may be a kayak. The kayak is ideal for nonmotorized, short-distance, shallow-draft, and deep channel-crossing situations. In the past, kayaks simply did not have the necessary design and onboard features to satisfy a flats fisherman's needs. The last few years have changed all that. Major manufacturers offer fully rigged flats fishing vessels with state-of-the-art technology and necessary features like rod holders, bait storage, stowed storage compartments, and so much more.

In essence, kayaks are the bridge between wading and using a poled, motorized flats boat. The easily maneuvered human-powered kayak offers low-profile stealth while avoiding the leg fatigue and possible physical vulnerability that may accompany wading. To reach a tailing

The kayak revolution comes to Florida redfish country. Photo by Heritage Kayaks.

bonefish on a Key Largo flat, you might need to wade a hundred yards or more. With a kayak, you can effortlessly paddle right up to these fish.

Flats Boats

The next tier of necessity is a motorized, shallow-draft vessel. The means of propulsion is not a paddle but a graphite or fiberglass push-pole—hence, the term *poling skiff* is often used to refer to a flats boat.

With a poling skiff, you are dependent on an outboard motor for traveling from port to the flats and back again. Although the quality of outboard marine motors has never been higher, you will need to service your motor. Unlike certain wilderness flats destinations outside the United States, Florida is equipped with the best of marinas, fuel, accessories, and service centers to help you keep your boat and motor in optimal condition.

Among flats boats there are two subcategories of craft designed to meet specific needs. To determine the exact type of flats boat you

The deletion of a center console, plus a lightweight outboard engine, makes this already shallow-floating boat even lighter. Photo by Ranger Boats.

This is a standard layout flats boat often seen in Florida. It has an engine jack plate and recessed trim tabs for better shallow water running capability. Photo by Ranger Boats.

will need, consider the species you are seeking, the depth of the water where your prey will be, and the type of water you will be crossing to reach them. For instance, fishing the shallow mudflats in front of Flamingo, Florida, for five-pound tailing redfish necessitates a different flats boat than running from Key West to the Marquesas to fish for twenty-pound permit in four feet of water.

Flats boats of the first subcategory float in the shallowest of waters. This class of flats boat is where all of the latest technological action is taking place. Many of these boats are being built with a "vacuum bag" technology, which creates a solidly constructed vessel of very light weight, sometimes only four hundred pounds. These boats are able to float in as little as four or five inches of water and are quite capable of being poled right up to tailing bonefish and redfish. This is useful in the shallowest flats, like Florida's Flamingo, Pine Island Sound, the Indian River, and northeast Florida Bay.

Many of these ultrashallow flats boats need only a small outboard engine because of their hull's light weight. They also sport lower freeboard, closely approaching the advantages of a kayak in unobtrusiveness. These boats offer minimal hull slap, low profile, extremely shallow draft, and are operated from either a tiller handle engine or a heavier center console and helm. Such skiffs generally run in size from fourteen to sixteen feet, although there are exceptions.

The other subcategory of flats boats is the more traditional mainstay of Florida flats fishing—the skiffs that have been around the state for the last thirty years. Although the cockpit layout is basically the same as in the newer, lighter flats boats, these skiffs feature center console operation—in part because their heavier hulls and larger size call for bigger and heavier outboard motors. These boats generally run from sixteen to nineteen feet in length. They have the higher freeboard and deeper V-shaped bottom configurations necessary for crossing larger, weather-intensive waters and for handling larger flats species like sharks, tarpon, and barracuda. They offer a bit more "angler enclosure" and heavier hull stability.

Some of these boats have rod storage racks inside or below the gunwales, and almost all standard flats skiffs have some vertical rod storage in tubes affixed to the center console. The important thing about flats boat tackle storage is that gear be out of the way—particularly

This flats boat also has the additional features of an electric trolling motor and stern anchoring device. Photo by Ranger Boats.

when the active tackle is fly tackle—yet still be convenient enough at hand to grab for a shot at an approaching flats fish that necessitates another type of presentation.

Some of the important features to look for in all flats boats are clear, uncluttered fore and aft casting decks, lots of flush storage compartments with drainable rain gutters, retractable pushpole holders for fly fishing, recessed running lights, release and livewells featuring pumped-in water, or an aft livewell drilled for unpumped seawater.

All flats boats should have a poling tower over the engine to help the poler spot fish for the angler fishing off the bow. Certain flats boats have an elevated removable platform for the angler in the bow. This is helpful to see approaching permit and tarpon on deeper flats, but is not necessary for shallow flats and tailing fish. My skiff also has a center console that features a VHF radio, lots of storage, and a depth recorder to spot honeyholes in the flats drop-offs. All flats boats should be fitted with trim tabs at the transom for optimal vessel performance.

Both classes of flats boats offer some models of extreme shallow water running capability. This is achieved by the use of jack plates,

This is a large flats boat with real open water capability. Photo by Ranger Boats.

which lift the engine vertically while the vessel is under way, thereby reducing draft. The engine is "fed" with salt water by lowered water intakes and by a pocket cut into the boat's transom bottom that throws water back and up at the spinning prop so that it has something to "bite into." In addition, many Florida anglers utilize a four-bladed prop to give the lower unit more teeth to bite into the thrown-up water. With these features, many of the ultrashallow flats boats can literally run in water less than twelve inches deep. Although this has great logistical utility, it is my belief that running the flats is a destructive practice that will drive Florida flats fish off their accustomed feeding habitat and risk tearing up seagrasses. If you need to get to the next flat, pole or electric-motor your vessel into deeper water and use those depths for your travel. Avoid running our precious Florida flats!

When choosing between a kayak and a flats boat, various features and characteristics should be considered. While a flats boat risks spooking more fish because of having a higher profile, more hull slap, and a greater pressure wave than a kayak, it offers more physical enclosure and personal safety. Although the kayak will never replace the flats boat in all situations, it may prove to be a more effective choice in some circumstances. Consider the following:

1. Kayaks are dependent on human paddle power; flats boats require an engine.
2. Kayaks can cross channels too deep for a pushpole to reach without resorting to firing up an engine.
3. Kayaks often weigh less than one hundred pounds, a mere fraction of what most flats boats and engines weigh.
4. Because of their light weight, kayaks draw less water than most flats boats.
5. A kayak can traverse the softest flats bottoms better because it is paddled over the bottom rather than being propelled by a pole pushed against the soft bottom.
6. Kayaks offer a lower profile than flats boats because the angler maintains a sitting position. It is not necessary to be up high to spot, approach, and pursue a tailing fish.
7. Because of a kayak's light weight, you can easily tow it around by a belt attachment.
8. Because of its low profile, a kayak can penetrate and travel through mangrove cover.
9. Kayaks are much more vulnerable to strong winds and high waves than are flats boats.
10. Kayaks are not capable of jumping up on a plane and attaining the high speeds that a motorized flats boat may need in certain situations, as when fleeing a lightning-throwing squall or getting an injured person to port or a mothership.
11. Kayaks do not have the dry storage, livewell, rod storage, or accessory potential of a flats boat, although they have more features now than ever before.

Bay Boats

Like kayaks, bay boats are a newer development than the standard Florida flats boat. I consider them the third tier of necessity in flats fishing, but they are also a tier of opportunity. Bay boats generally run from about eighteen feet to well over twenty feet. They truly qualify

This is a standard bay boat. Note that there is no pushpole. Photo by Ranger Boats.

for offshore and reef fishing but are capable of being utilized in many flats fishing applications. Unlike flats boats, bay boats generally use a bow-mounted electric motor as the propulsion while hunting on the flats. Some bay boats, however, feature pushpole storage or holders for those just-in-case situations. Think of the marvelous possibilities: perhaps you are off Everglades City and want to fish a permit wreck thirty miles offshore in the morning, then run back and fish the back-country flats for snook late in the afternoon. If you have a bay boat, all of this is possible in one day in the same vessel.

In actuality, a bay boat often looks like a giant flats boat. Unlike the twenty-five-foot center consoles that have dominated the Key West fishing scene, bay boats feature lower freeboard, flats-boat-style casting decks and cockpits, and a bottom configuration that actually allows some of these vessels to float in just over a foot of water. Yet their large size allows the use of engines of two hundred horsepower or more, which makes offshore fishing with a bay boat a realistic and quite safe proposition. Captain Tom Rowland has had great success using his bay boat for offshore trips and incredibly successful permit trips on the flats—all on the same day—off Key West and the lower Florida Keys (see chapter 8).

Wade, Kayak, Pole, or Troll

In reality, these tiers of necessity are often blended. Anglers often use a flats boat for transportation and then get out of the boat to wade after their flats species target. I routinely use my sixteen-foot flats boat to get me to some flats in south Biscayne Bay, simply because I can't reach them by wading (or walking) to them. Once I get there, if my targets are big tailing bonefish on a hard wadable bottom, I almost always anchor my skiff and wade to them.

Florida has such a marvelous diversity of flats habitat. As a flats hunter, you will choose the method of pursuit that best realizes your angling dreams. From the shallow creeks of the First Coast to the flats of the Keys to the shallows off the Big Bend, you can wade, kayak, pole, or troll.

This is a large bay boat with a center console tee top. Photo by Ranger Boats.

5

Florida Weather on the Flats

A comprehensive weather check should be standard operating procedure before any flats fishing outing: first for your personal safety, and second because the weather determines what, when, and where you will be fishing on the flats.

In the past, you may have done a number of things to check the weather: take a look outside, tune into the Weather Channel on television, or check out the Weather Service on your VHF radio. These activities are informative; however, a thorough weather check requires a computer with Internet access and a visit to some National Oceanic and Atmospheric Administration (NOAA) data. My personal preference is to start my data gathering on the Web site for the National Weather Service Forecast Office for my "start area," which is Miami–South Florida. You can access the homepage for the Florida area you will be flats fishing by typing it into the search field on the top toolbar.

The Internet address or URL for Miami–South Florida is http://www.srh.noaa.gov/mfl. Find the URL for a Florida city close to the flats you plan on fishing. If it is an area you fish often, perhaps you will want to bookmark this page or place it among your favorites for easy access in the future.

Although the NOAA Web site may undergo changes through time, it will likely retain essential features and categories that can help you plan your fishing day.

Specific information to look for includes:

- A local forecast, including the forecast at-a-glance for seven days, hazardous weather outlook, and current radar and satellite images.
- Current hazards, which may include watches, warnings, and advisories for lightning, tornadoes, fires, or floods; during hurricane season (June through November), look for a tropics or hurricane section, which will give the status and projected path of impending storms.
- Current conditions, including "sky weather," air temperature, wind direction and speed, barometric pressure, and lunar phase.
- Satellite images of static and moving weather systems in black and white and color over the state of Florida.
- Radar images providing a "real time" sweep over Florida for rain activity.
- Offshore and beach marine forecasts, tidal times and heights, and graphic forecasts that show projected water temperatures and wind direction and speed over Florida waters.

Seasonal Preferences of Fish Species

Florida is considered to have a subtropical yet temperate climate. It does not have the climactic constancy of equatorial tropical islands like Christmas Island or Fanning Island in the South Pacific. These latter destinations are atolls that have regular balmy weather and minor tidal fluctuations and therefore offer a year-round bonefishery.

In contrast, Florida's more northerly position on our planet and its attachment to the North American landmass make it quite vulnerable to regular cold fronts from late fall through the winter and well into spring. While Florida's tides are not extreme, its wide variation of temperature from month to month necessitates that flats fishermen choose specific months and seasons of the year for the best flats fishing results.

It is fair to say that Florida flats fishing is best when the weather is pleasant, balmy, and warm. These conditions make it most likely that our major flats species will be up on the flats and feeding. Conversely, during a fierce cold front that drops water temperatures into the sixties, flats fish tend to drop off into the warmer and less disturbed depths of adjacent channels or offshore waters. Flats fish can be caught during cold weather, but at such times the fishery is less consistent and less predictable.

One of the quickest ways to get a basic fix on the seasonal and water temperature tolerances of the major flats species is to look at their geographical distribution. The species that flourish in the northernmost Florida flats and the sounds, bays, and beaches of North Carolina are the spotted seatrout and the redfish (or channel bass). In contrast, more truly tropical flats species like permit, snook, and tarpon are rarely found or fished outside the warmer waters of Florida. Florida is a fingerlike temperature-moderating peninsula that thrusts itself into the waters of the Atlantic Ocean, the warm Gulf Stream current, the Gulf of Mexico, and the Florida Straits.

Hurricanes and Flats Fishing

No discussion of Florida weather and its influence on flats fishing would be complete without an examination of hurricanes. Simply put, a hurricane is a tropical cyclone that starts as an area of disturbed, low-pressure weather and consolidates into the dreaded spinning pinwheel we know all too well. The Florida hurricane season is approximately June through November, when the warm atmospheric conditions and warm ocean water that fuel these storms are present. Accordingly, hurricanes gain strength and consolidate over warm open ocean water and lose strength and dissipate over land.

Post-Storm Assessments

The flats of Florida—because of their extremely shallow depth—can be highly impacted by hurricanes. The extent of the impact is contingent on many factors: the actual material of the flats bottom; the storm's track, strength, and duration; and the location of the eye of the storm relative to the flat, which will determine wind direction.

According to one of Sanibel Island's top flats guides, Captain Mike Smith, the interior flats of Pine Island Sound experienced some rearrangement by Hurricane Charley in 2004. He feels this occurred because the soft muddy material that composed the flats bottom of the area made it more subject to changes by the storm. In addition, the open expanse of the area allowed top hurricane winds to prevail for hours over the extremely shallow flats. Captain Mike observed that the hurricane displaced the soft bottom into channels that held flats fish (like snook and redfish) and covered up some of the shallow trenches that flats fish had been using for exit and entry. The storm also destroyed some shoreline trees that the fish used for ambush cover.

The Atlantic side of the Florida Keys provides a somewhat different hurricane-to-flats-bottom relationship. A good deal of this flats bottom on the ocean side is reef or hard sand attached to and abutting the actual limestone of the Florida Keys. Under equal hurricane conditions, these types of flats tend to maintain themselves better than the interior soft-bottomed backcountry flats of Florida Bay. Interestingly, the shelled life forms that are food to certain flats fish may be more vulnerable to a hurricane's turbulence over the hard bottoms. When storm winds blow the backcountry soft flats around, food species, such as clams, are merely folded back into the mud rather than "flushed out," as occurs over the hard-bottomed ocean flats.

You'll recall that hurricanes also change their intensity based on whether they are over land, the temperature of the water they are over, and the condition of the hurricane's eye—as the eyewall evolves through the replacement cycle. For instance, sea-heated hurricane Wilma in 2005 roared into the Yucatan Peninsula—and its countless flats—as a Category 5 storm packing 150-mile-per-hour winds. It hovered over the area for an agonizing two days, wreaking havoc. Wilma weakened to Category 1 strength because of friction with the Yucatan. As the storm headed toward Florida, it was recharged by the warm Loop Current into a Category 3 storm, packing 125-mile-per-hour winds that smashed into the shallows off Everglades City. An approaching trough and cold front picked up the storm and slingshot it northeast and across the state in just six hours. Although Florida suffered terribly, it is likely that the flats of the Yucatan suffered more.

It is common practice to assess a hurricane's track, strength, and duration when making weather projections and assessing one's safety on land. The storm's eye location is important because the eye of the storm has the strongest winds, and the position of the eye determines the direction of the winds. Locating the "dirty" side of the hurricane is prudent, because it is the most active part of the storm.

Try to visualize how all these factors combine to affect not just the flats but also the fish themselves, both predator and prey. For instance, a hurricane makes landfall on a series of Florida's flats. Depending on the track and the eye position, a massive inshore storm surge and fierce wind can send a tsunami-like wall of water over the flats, transforming shoal waters into a dirty bay. As the storm and its eyewall pass, the winds may switch to an opposing quadrant and literally cause the deeply flooded flats to be emptied out by a monstrously powerful wind-created ebb tide. Alternatively, again depending on the storm's and the eye's positions, a hurricane can flood some flats while emptying out others on the opposite side of its center.

For your safety, wait at least a week or two after the storm has passed before initiating poststorm explorations. Dangerous debris in the water—both visible and submerged—can cause damage to your flats vessel. The only vessels that were capable of entering the "urban asphalt flats" of post-Katrina New Orleans were airboats and flats boats. In addition, the waters may stay dirty for up to two weeks or more. Running your skiff through dirty seawater and across shoaled-over flats is a recipe for disaster. Explore poststorm flats slowly and carefully!

Hurricane Effects on Flats Fish and Their Prey

The next determination is assessing hurricane effects on the flats fish and their food sources. The major effect is generally displacement. Loads of flats fish feed in Florida's shallows during the summer and early fall months, which coincide with the hurricane season. Sometime during almost every twenty-four hours of those months, the warm waters are user-friendly for all major flats species. It is fair to assume that flats fish sense the approach of the storm through dropping atmospheric pressure and growing storm effects. Inevitably, they leave the flats for deeper water in the channels or the sea, where the storm effects are moderated. We know these movements have utility, because it is unusual to find large-scale kills of tarpon, bonefish, permit, or other flats fish after the passage of a hurricane.

Regardless of the deeper water refuges, the high winds and storm surges with huge water volume shifts are sure to create short-lived disorientation and hesitance for flats fish. In addition, if the hurricane is also a major rain event, you can expect the freshwater drainage from both the land and the South Florida Water Management District canals to send a huge plume of dirty fresh water out across some of the flats. This will have the biggest negative effect on highly saline species like bonefish and barracuda, and a diminished though measurable effect on species that thrive in brackish water, like snook, tarpon, and redfish. With all these changes to cope with, flats fish may show the caution and disorientation of any displaced life-form.

Because the major food sources for flats fish occupy the bottom, strong hurricanes that shift bottom matter can have a displacing effect on the flats bottom biomass. Three weeks after the 1992 passage of Hurricane Andrew—a viciously destructive storm—I snorkeled and explored some rock pile crevices off the Ragged Keys. I found these permit hot spots to be devoid of the usual black sea urchins, hermit crabs, and small lobsters that usually live there year-round. After that offshore look around, I took advantage of the high tide to pole my skiff to the outside shorelines of these keys and snorkel that area. It was immediately apparent that there was no shortage of these food sources along the shorelines. I theorized that the huge storm surge to these barrier keys flushed the life-forms out of the rock piles into the shoreline. The best poststorm flats fishing approach is to understand that action and results may come from entirely new places.

Thunderstorms and Flats Fishing

The Sunshine State has no shortage of thunderstorms. It is important to understand these weather events; they affect flats anglers and also anyone else who is outdoors and at risk. Thunderstorms can be associated with cold fronts or hurricanes, or they can occur as summertime entities unto themselves. The latter type is the most common occurrence. Thunderstorms are born of rising, unstable, hot, moist air

A mothership is always handy, since it provides a "portable port." This is especially important in foul weather. Photo by Scott Heywood/Angling Destinations.

that uses water vapor as fuel. A frequent manifestation of a Florida thunderstorm comes during the summertime when the late afternoon inland landmass—which is generally warmer than the coast—gives off rising hot air that mushrooms into a thunderstorm. Not uncommonly, these storms proceed seaward with varying amounts and intensity of rain, thunder, and lightning. Eventually, they seem to spend themselves and the summertime evening is quiet, peaceful, and fresh smelling.

Another less common thunderstorm scenario occurs on the Atlantic side of Florida, where the offshore Gulf Stream features warmer air temperatures in the deep of night than over the adjacent cooler landmass. These conditions can give rise to offshore thunderstorms at dawn that are "burnt off" by the rising sun. In the right conditions, thunderstorms can occur at any time of day and in multiple locations. As an angler, you do not have to be a meteorologist, but you need a rudimentary understanding of the causes and behavior of thunderstorms in Florida—not just for your angling effectiveness but for your survival.

Like hurricanes, thunderstorms often pose more of a threat to fishermen than to fish. While all anglers flee a hurricane, some anglers play risky games with thunderstorms. The rule should be clear—if you experience thunder, lightning, waterspouts, or increased wind velocity, leave the area immediately! A better approach is to anticipate a thunderstorm while it is being formed: learn the difference between a light, dispersed shower and a potentially towering cumulus cloud. The crux of this craft is to recognize when a cloud "goes bad." Another skill is to go beyond an assessment of a cloud's vertical development and work up a sensitivity to the path of a developed thunderstorm. The

Fair weather gives anglers good overhead light and increases their ability to spot cruising fish. Photo by Scott Heywood/Angling Destinations.

Calm water at dawn and dusk can make these times great for tailing fish. Photo by Scott Heywood/Angling Destinations.

Keep a careful eye on thunderstorms and have an exit plan. Photo by Scott Heywood/Angling Destinations.

steering currents aloft that push a thunderstorm may not be the same as the winds you are feeling on the water thousands of feet below the storm.

Watch suspicious clouds carefully for any darkening, towering, flattening cloud belly, lightning, thunder, or waterspouts. If any of these phenomena are present, make like a zoot-suited hipster—"later, daddy-o"—and split! Once a thunderstorm is upon you, potentially torrential rain can block your navigated exit. In a thunderstorm, being hit by lightning becomes a real threat—why take the chance? If you get caught, put on the rain jacket that is a standard part of your gear and remove potential lightning attractors like fishing rods from the vertical console or the holders on your poling tower.

This type of weather event seems to produce widely varying effects among the flats fish species—and widely varying opinions among expert flats guides and anglers. I have caught bonefish after the passing of some long vicious thunderstorms. I fled the flat well before the storm arrived, watched the storm pass over, and returned to the area when the coast was clear. My experience with tarpon on Florida's flats has been less reliable: as long as it simply showered, the fish continued to roll and come by in strings. If the shower morphed into a thunderstorm with lightning, "boomers," and rapid drops in air temperature, the tarpon most often went off the feed. Interestingly, my experience with small tarpon laid up in a few feet of water alongside mangroves has been much more reliable after thunderstorms. Shallow water snook also seem more resilient when they are near or under mangroves as a thunderstorm arrives. Other flats guides and fishermen may have tales to tell about their experiences with each of the flats species, but I cannot contribute any experience whatsoever regarding flats fish behavior *during* a thunderstorm.

The Cold Front Phenomenon

The discussion of bonefish (chapter 6) includes some detail about cold fronts, but a great deal more remains to be said. Like other weather events, cold fronts are highly individual in their characteristics. An assessment of the front's intensity, duration, and potential contrast to the preexisting air mass over Florida is useful in predicting the likely effects of a front on your local flats fishing.

All Florida residents and many visitors are familiar with cold fronts. They are natural phenomena like thunderstorms and hurricanes. Cold fronts are generally not a threat to property or life, as hurricanes are and thunderstorms can be. Nevertheless, on occasion cold fronts can be both massive and ferocious.

A cold front's leading chilly edge and body bring changes to the prevailing air and water temperatures. The precise nature of those changes is determined by the front's intensity and duration. For instance, a powerful cold front that lasts for days will feature strong, shifting winds over Florida's flats and a drop in the seawater temperature. Severe fronts generally create more repellent conditions to Florida's flats fish than do mild fronts. On occasion, a severe winter front can bunch up bonefish on the ocean side of the upper Florida Keys.

Early Fronts and Early Parts of Fronts

The first fronts of the year usually begin in late October and signal the advent of the fall season and the eventual unfolding of winter sometime in December. People new to Florida should understand that South Florida is somewhat tropical and therefore features more subtle seasonal changes than in the state's northern reaches. The early fronts of fall draw mixed reviews from different species of flats fish and different categories of flats fishermen.

These early fronts bring an end to the dog days of summer: the humid, seemingly endless days of scalding heat give way to cooler weather and slowly dropping water temperatures. Species that favor temperate weather, like seatrout and bonefish, respond with vigor to the cooling waters of early fall, which descend right into their temperature tolerance and feeding ranges. It seems like magic the way these species reappear on the Florida flats in large numbers comparable to those of the prior spring.

In contrast, tropical species like snook and tarpon do quite well in warm water and start to get uncomfortable on Florida's flats when cold fronts drop the water temperatures below seventy-five degrees. Permit are somewhat "tropical" on the flats; they, too, will start to leave the flats when cold fronts start to plunge the waters down into the low seventies and high sixties. All of these species respond negatively to cooler water pervading the flats, yet their responses are species specific. Species like snook, which thrive in brackish mangroves, will go into "transition mode," moving more deeply inshore in sheltered rivers, hot water discharges, and sun-responsive and sheltered mainland mudflats. Very large snook may seek the shelter of deeper offshore structures. Mature tarpon often take up residence on the warm bottom thermoclines of ocean inlets. Permit, in contrast to bonefish and snook, spend the bulk of their Florida summer over rubble-reef flats. As the early fronts start to blow, permit make their way to deep offshore structures like wrecks. It is useful to have a keen sense of the temperature tolerance range of each flats species.

Cold fronts over Florida have to travel over a huge landmass in order to cover the state completely. The long north-south peninsula begins on the temperate Georgia border and peters out in subtropical Key West; it therefore has gradations of climate zones. Another aspect of a cold front you should assess is its reach, meaning how far its intensity or momentum will take it. You have perhaps heard of fronts "stalling" halfway down the state. Consult all NOAA electronic sources, your local and state weather forecasts, and the NOAA Web Site (www.srh.noaa.gov). If you find that your redfish trip to the Banana River might be blasted by a cold front forecast to stall over Clewiston, switch your flats fishing trip to Key West, and go and catch a big, silvery permit.

The Early Front and Fishing Tactics

A cold front enters Florida as a chilly wedge of air from the north or northwest and will clash and interact with a prevailing warmer air mass. Some cold fronts that enter Florida on the heels of a prior front have less contrast with the prevailing air mass, and less of a clashing effect. Often, the beginning of the front and its leading edge may have some disturbed weather featuring clouds and showers. The previously clearer skies become opaque and overcast, which lowers the overhead light and makes it more difficult to see through the water to spot cruising fish. This may be accompanied by winds shifting into the southwest or west. As long as the water temperature remains at a friendly level for your species of flats fish—use a thermometer, not your hand—this might be a good time to pursue tailing or waking bonefish or redfish on a lee side flat that is shallow or has a falling tide.

During the first part of a front, I have experienced good bonefishing on the mainland side of Biscayne Bay and respectable redfishing among the more sheltered northern islands of Florida Bay. This illustrates that being tucked away from the westerly winds and the passing light showers may mean that an angler can still see tailing fish. However, severe fronts—even in their early stages—bring the intensified wind, rain, and temperature conditions that flats fish find repellent.

Perhaps you have heard about anglers and guides observing flats fish feeding aggressively before a cold front. Some people theorize that the fish (for instance, bonefish) are stoking up in anticipation of bad weather in a "nuts-for-the-winter" fashion. The truth is that it is unlikely for bonefish to behave in the same way people do when they store food, water, medicine, gas, and a generator in anticipation of a hurricane. There are other ways to understand this observation. First and foremost, bonefish feed all the time, perhaps even better in the windiest conditions, provided that the water temperature is adequate. Second, it is not unusual for some wind activity to occur before a front. Wind roils the surface, and bonefish are a bit less cautious—baits, lures, and flies can hit the water more noisily, and the wind will cushion the sound. Winds help dislodge and disorient bottom-dwelling biomass, giving the bonefish better feeding opportunities. Yet it is also true that flats fish stop feeding as a cold front approaches. The best way to take on the Florida flats as a cold front is approaching is to be scientific, which means keeping a totally open mind. Follow what the fish are doing, not what you think they should be doing.

The Mature Front

A mature front displays characteristic china blue skies and cold air blowing from a northerly quadrant over Florida waters. The sky sports a different atmosphere—the light is bright, radiant, and prevalent. The sun shines unobstructed by clouds from the blue dome above. At this stage of a mature front, you are on a seesaw: visibility through the flats water column is excellent, yet the cold air that accompanies these conditions is dropping the water temperature and driving fish away. Strong fronts (bringing air temperatures down to sixty degrees or less) of long duration (three or more days) will drop the water temperatures significantly. The front that shoved Hurricane Wilma across Florida in 2005 dropped water temperatures from eighty-three to seventy-nine degrees in four days. Each additional day the front remains will take the water temperature lower. Because water temperature changes more slowly than air temperature, the first day of a front might still translate into warm enough water for flats fish, provided that the water was warm enough to begin with. As the water temperature drops, keep in mind the temperature tolerance ranges of each individual flats species. If I am fishing the Lower Keys backcountry during day two or day three of a moderate cold front, I focus my efforts on flats barracuda rather than bonefish, tarpon, or permit.

As the front completes its progression, the winds go from north to northeast, to east, and back to the prevailing southeast and puffy cumulus clouds. If the trade wind pattern stays in effect long enough—with no interrupting fronts—the water temperature climbs on the flats, and the flats fish return to the shallows in accordance with their individual water temperature needs.

Cold Front Reminders for Flats Fishermen

Fish are cold-blooded. As the water temperature drops, so does their level of metabolic activity. During a cold front, pick the warmest conditions, such as afternoons; shallow, muddy, heat-retaining flats; and flats adjacent to deeper, warmer water. No doubt you will dress in layers to deal with the daily frontal temperature changes during your flats fishing trip—flats fish do not have that luxury. The warmest areas of the flats are havens for them.

When I fish on Florida's flats during a mature front, I slow down my retrieves and use smaller lures and flies. I also use the lightest possible fluorocarbon tippets or leaders. Cold flats fish are generally hesitant feeders when they are out of their usual preferred temperatures, so they need a little stimulation. I use live crabs, shrimp, whitebait, or small mullet if necessary to do the job.

Bonefish

With Tim Borski

COCHRAN

Illustration by Vaughn Cochran

Bonefish (*Albula vulpes*)
Size Range: 3 to 16 pounds
Florida State Record: 15 pounds, 12 ounces
Florida Habitat: Shallow flats from Key Biscayne to Key West
Baits: Shrimp, crabs, small jigs, and flies
Tackle: 8-pound spinning; 8-weight fly
Bonefish Hot Spots: The trophy bonefish of your dreams are often found on
the flats around Islamorada in the Florida Keys.

The predawn is still and humid. To the east over Indian Key, the first hint of the sunrise begins as a yellow and blue barred arc.

It is a peaceful time. You can hear the liquid whoosh of your skiff as your guide poles you forward. He is your gray ghost gondolier.

In this sauna-like moment, you feel dawn's ambient heat begin to break a sweat on your body. As the sun rises, the low tide flat in front of you takes on clarity: shapes and shadows become detailed. You begin to make out a big heron in the two o'clock position about 150 feet away.

A dragonfly hums alongside the skiff, and with a quick turn settles on your rod tip—perhaps gaining a moment's respite from flying in all this summer swelter. Your new companion has grabbed your attention, which is a focus you can ill afford. With tolerant amusement, you shake your rod. The dislodged stowaway flies off in the twelve o'clock direction, right off the bow tip.

As you watch it vanish into the horizon, suddenly, just below it, you spot a tail breaking the surface along the edge of some knee-high mangroves. The tail drops down into the stillness and everything seems to stop . . . but five seconds and a thousand heartbeats later, it pops up again and your breathing resumes.

A few flicks of the tail take it into a slice of sunlight beaming through the greenery. The tail takes on a bright silver color. You get the brief impression that last night's crescent moon dropped down for a well-needed swim after a long night aloft. Now that you know it is not a phantom fish, but the real McCoy, you want to tell your guide.

Suddenly the skiff shoves forward and you struggle not to stumble: small sounds get big in a great calm expanse. You turn around for a look to see what's up with your guide, and when you see his eyes, it is clear he sees the fish. Without even a glance your way, he hisses: "Turn around and keep your eyes on the fish!"

His admonition snaps you back to reality like the shock of ice water to a boxer between rounds. You realize once again you are in Islamorada, the Madison Square Garden of trophy bonefishing. From behind you, your guide whispers: "He's really big, well over twelve pounds." You take a very deep breath, knowing that in no time at all you will be arriving at the moment of truth.

Off to the right, the heron grows restless at your approach. With a loud croak, it crouches, surges airborne, and takes flight. It banks to the left, coming across your bow—and right over the big bonefish you have been stalking. The fish reacts to the feathered 747 overhead with a huge splash. Suddenly it is swimming briskly to the channel; the bulge of its wake looks enormous. A few more seconds and the wake disappears. As you gaze across the perfectly flat, featureless surface of the water, all you can hear is your rapid breathing and pounding heart. Welcome to the world of bonefishing, my friend!

The Florida Bonefish

All too rarely does flats fishing literature focus on the Florida bonefish per se, yet I feel that this is the fish that has been the source of one of the most explosively growing inshore marine sport fisheries. More often, you will read tales about hordes of gullible bonefish that grab your fly only a rod's length away on the sandflats of some faraway exotic island. All this spin only proves that the term *adventure* is relative. Some anglers jet across the globe to the Indian Ocean or South Pacific to pursue unpressured bonefish. They travel thousands of miles and spend thousands of dollars. For me, adventure consists of hunting down, casting to, battling, and releasing some of the smartest bonefish in the world—the gray ghosts of Miami to Key West.

The bonefish of Florida are utterly fascinating and distinctive compared to other bonefish populations around the world. One of the major attractions of Florida bonefish is their enormous average size and size range. Our bonefish average six or seven pounds and have been caught weighing over fifteen pounds. It is fair to say that Florida bonefish are some of the largest of this species on the entire planet. My research indicates that other destinations, like Bimini, New Caledonia, Christmas Island, or the Seychelles, do not offer the regularity and results *per unit of effort* for catching large bonefish that Florida does.

In addition, I believe no other destination allows an angler to catch a trophy bonefish so economically. When I began my flats fishing in the sixties, I routinely waded the oceanside flats from north Key

Largo to Marathon in the Florida Keys. As I drove down from Miami, I would test the volume limits of my radio with songs by the Four Seasons, Bobby Vee, and Gene Pitney. These tunes became associated with soon-to-be-waded limestone flats under a bright and bold Florida sun. It became clear that certain flats had larger bonefish than others, and I focused on these areas. As a wader, gaining access to certain flats became an art form to me. By the time the bell-bottomed seventies arrived, I had lost count of the bonefish over nine pounds I'd caught and released by simply wading from the roadside—and all it took was the cost of gasoline to get me there. I am proud to live in a state that can lay claim to that type of bonefishing.

Bonefish Characteristics

The bonefish is the prototypical flats fish. Its adult life revolves around the flats and shallows from Key Biscayne in Miami to Key West. When other glamorous species appear on the flats, this does not necessarily imply that they live there. Consider the other two of the "Big Three": permit spend a good deal of their time offshore, "holding" over structure. Tarpon often travel across hundreds of miles of open ocean before reaching the flats. Even large broodstock redfish have been encountered far offshore in the Gulf of Mexico. Although research posits that larval and tiny bonefish may involve offshore waters as part of their growth cycle, it remains possible that their whole life cycle could occur in the inshore shallows. Whatever future research discovers, the Florida bonefish is flats fish incarnate—the ruling king of the shallows.

Bonefish are extremely diverse and versatile in the ways they travel and feed along the flats. In addition, their bullet-train battling style is never forgotten. Although they do not make the missile leaps of barracuda or the head-shaking jumps of tarpon, hooked bonefish probably have the fastest initial run of any flats fish. Bonefish manifest themselves in more ways than most other Florida flats fish. They are a joy to watch as they tail up around the low tide—it is particularly easy to see them on overcast days. Take off your sunglasses and do not look through the water. Simply watch for the tails and dorsal fins as they break the water surface. Keep the same strategies in mind for spotting "waking" bonefish as they make moving bulges on the water surface as they travel. Be sure to cast well ahead of the wake, because the tails of the fish are creating the water disturbance, not their heads. Tailing bonefish are feeding—not traveling—and may require a closer, but very delicate, presentation.

For the other ways these fish are found on the flats, you want excellent overhead light to help you see through the water to spot them. Put your sunglasses back on as you spot for bonefish (singly or in groups) cruising along the bottom, as they churn up mud while foraging on soft bottoms, or perhaps when they follow a stingray, looking for a freebie flushed-out meal. On special occasions, you will be delighted to see them surface while spawning on an oceanside wintertime flat, or perhaps they will come up to sip a silver minnow cocktail.

I propose a toast—yes, again!—to the unique strength of bonefish when they are hooked and making their initial run. Whoever would think that line could rip through the ultrashallow water like some cosmic force ripping a vast tropical envelope in half? On the sprint, they appear to be the strongest pound-for-pound fighter on the flats. One of my mentors, a college teacher, once gave me a multiple-choice pop quiz. Perhaps you can try it. You are armed with an eight-weight fly rod or an eight-pound spinner and you hook:

(a) a ten-pound redfish
(b) a ten-pound tarpon
(c) a ten-pound bonefish
(d) a ten-pound permit

Which fish would you expect to torment your tackle the most on its initial runs? Other notables like Caesar and Damon Runyan might simply say: "Tie them tail to tail and let the games begin!"

Bonefish Feeding Patterns and Tactics

At their most basic nature, bonefish are bottom feeders. Yet they are feeders of a very opportunistic type—they will consume small finfish, crustaceans, and shellfish with equal relish. They are able to eat hard-bodied life-forms because they possess hard throat crushers that pulverize the shells. This allows the inedible parts to be blown out by the bonefish, while they swallow the digestible, protein-rich meat and organ tissues. Their hard mouth and throat structures have relevance in your hooking tactics for the gray ghost. Try to strike your bonefish before it subjects your bait—either natural or artificial—to its crushing mechanism and spits out a crushed fly. Even live crab baits are easily pulverized and ejected. The best tactic with natural bait is to feel the weight of the fish as it turns away and strike firmly with the rod. With fly tackle, the only indication of a strike might be a tic or jump in the fly line, or just a twist of the bonefish's tail or dorsal fin. Assume that when the bonefish comes up to your fly, there will be a take. Keep your rod stationary and pointed straight at the fish; then strip-strike it. This strategy will also serve you well with permit because they, too, are armed with throat crushers.

Bonefish possess what fishery biologists call "site fidelity." This is an esoteric term that supports the idea that bonefish may live around and feed on a particular flat. If bonefish generally move onto the flat on a rising tide and off the flat on a falling tide and they have site fidelity, then eventually they will establish ways of traveling on a particular flat. These paths of travel are bottom contours like tiny cuts and bottom indentations that are often imperceptible to the angler's eye but are easily sensed by the bonefish. Maybe you have noticed that bonefish are distinct among flats fish in that evolution on the flats has given them an extra set of belly fins. These fins are extremely useful as water-level sensing and propulsion devices. The timing of when these travel routes are taken is triggered by the water level and direction of the current. Water level is often as important as tidal current, because a strong onshore wind can oppose a weak neap tide ebb current and keep water on the flat even if the tide is falling. This will prolong the time that grazing bonefish will remain on that flat.

Imagine your own human nature as you wander in the countryside and spot an apple tree in the middle of a small lake. You cannot tell how deep the surrounding water is unless you wade or swim through it. That makes you cautious, but those plump red apples make you hungry and you want to eat some. You look at the fruit tree again and see a small dry path that is basically linear—but slightly meandering—leading up to the fruit tree. Being a land-based life-form, you would be inclined to take the dry path. However, if that apple tree were surrounded by flat, dry land, the options for your path of approach would be different. Alternatively, if you explored the depth

The bonefish has large eyes and nares (nostrils), which help it to hunt down food effectively. Photo by Scott Heywood/Angling Destinations.

of the lake surrounding the apple tree and found it only ankle deep, that would also affect your approach options. Specifically, if the small dirt path were washed out, you would still learn that it was okay to get some apples in such easily traversed shallow water. This is a crude and simple example, but it illustrates the point that as water-based life-forms, bonefish learn the best ways of navigating the flats.

Bonefish therefore begin and hold to established travel routes on a flat that offers a good food supply. They also have an affinity for working certain bottom contours on any given flat. Some contours are well established—created by the ongoing confluence of tides, currents, winds, and bottom substrate. New contours are sometimes created by the passage of a tropical storm. After a contour rearrangement, bonefish may need time to reorient themselves and discover new travel paths. Other flats may be more uniform, and the bonefish simply spread out and feed meanderingly as the rising tide allows.

Every flat has its own unique characteristics and bonefish movement patterns. Study, fish, and learn each flat, and make notes and sketches so that you can refer to them the next time. Remember that flats can change over time, especially the sand-to-grass ratio after a hurricane; some flats are sandier and it takes a long period for the grass to grow back or to come up through the newly deposited, storm-piled sand. This makes a new flat that you may need to learn anew.

It is easy to tell how a fish species behaves simply by looking at it. Evolutionary changes derive from behavior effective for survival—as in the development of the giraffe's neck. Bonefish have huge eyes for excellent vision, superb nares for an excellent sense of smell, and a body and fin construction perfectly arranged for mobility and speed in very shallow water. They also have mirrorlike scales that are responsive to their surroundings, giving the fish the ability to change color to protect themselves. Overall, not such a bad "model" at first glance!

Chumming for Bonefish

Bonefish have more than adequate equipment for feeding—they feed with equal efficiency by sight or by smell. If they cannot see prey, they simply sniff it out. One of the more vivid examples I have seen of their highly developed sense of smell happened about ten years ago: the wind was over thirty miles per hour out of the east and the flats waters were clouded with sand. I had a guest from out of the country who begged me to go fishing in this mess, if we could go about it safely. I told him the only possibility was to hide behind Key Biscayne and blind-fish "behind chum," since the waters were colored like chocolate milk. These were hardly classic flats fishing prospects. He was absolutely ready to go and his desire to catch a bonefish was the priority—the method was secondary.

I fired up my engine and we eased our way through lumpy waves for about a mile. I could not see the bottom at all, but I was aware—as always—of the direction and stage of the tide. I slowed down where I thought a good spot on the flats would be. Next, a quick probe with my pushpole let me know we were in about three feet of water. I racked the pushpole and made the boat stationary with two sets of anchors off the stern, tying one off on each cleat, convinced I would need all this anchor power in such severe wind.

Using a Chum Tube

The next step was to break up some live shrimp and frozen squid and stuff them in my chum tube and Cuban yo-yo rig. A chum tube generally consists of a PVC tube about a foot long. The tube is drilled with as many holes as possible to let out the scent. The size of the holes should always be slightly smaller than the individual pieces of chum. The chum tube has threaded, removable caps at each end. One end is for the placement of fresh chum and replacement of washed-out foul chum. The other end of the chum tube has an eyelet that is attached to a throwing and retrieving device. The yo-yo is a donutlike plastic handline rig used for storing, throwing, and retrieving the line attached to the chum tube.

I asked my guest to watch where the chum tube landed and line up its landing with a shoreline structure to maintain an idea of its location—we certainly were not going to see the chum tube through the dirty water. We tossed out the tube and we both kept a good idea of its location as we baited up our eight-pound spinning rods with live shrimp. Because of the conditions, I explained how I would modify the shrimp. The water was turbid, so I wanted a very "smellable" live shrimp. First, I diced a live shrimp into chunks. I then slid one piece on each of the rigs up past the 2/0 hooks and over the double BB-sized split shots. After they were in place, I peeled a little piece of shell from one side of the tiny chunks—I wanted to give it more scent, yet keep it in place as a "nose hors d'oeuvre" on the doubled line.

Next I pinched the tail off the largest live shrimp and threaded them on the hooks, tail stump first. I wanted the largest shrimp—we were not casting, so I was not worried about a soft landing. I was basically trying to present to bonefish what they would sense as a large delicious meal, as when people are attracted by the wonderful aroma of something cooking in the kitchen. I am pleased to recollect that within a couple of minutes, we were both hooked up on rigs with drag that screamed out "bonefish." In all that wind, we fished for another two hours and caught five more bonefish. This type of a short trip illustrated with clarity how undaunted bonefish are by rough, dirty water. They simply transfer the power from sight to smell and feed on.

Many guides and anglers believe that bonefish can smell certain life forms that are buried under the sand. Once they get over the target area, they tip down and try to unearth this prey by blowing a jet of water from their mouths, or by actually rooting in the bottom with their snouts. A bonefish expects that its prey will be in survival mode, fleeing into cover or sand or remaining perfectly still. If the prey has weaponry, it may strike a defensive pose. Blue crabs, which abound on the bonefish flats from Miami to Key West, may attempt all three techniques when they are confronted by bonefish or humans. Yet bonefish prey will not actively attack bonefish: running or hiding are their primary modes of survival. Therefore, your flies and artificials should match the hatch not only in appearance but also in retrieve style and depth.

With bonefish, you will work the bottom the vast majority of times. With permit, I have been successful retrieving a bucktail or fly to get the fish's attention, then letting it drop to the bottom perfectly still and await the pickup. With bonefish, however, the opposite is more effective: a still lure or fly that suddenly announces its sandy hideaway with a puff of movement. On the off chance that you encounter bonefish chasing glass minnows on the surface, you can make a mid-surface to surface retrieve. Remember to let the fish turn away with your minnow fly before you strike it. Learn to study the behaviors of bonefish prey as you wade or pole the flats—your success rate will soar. Another way to assess "bonefishability" indirectly on a new flat or a known flat under different conditions is to look for visible signs of life, such as worm mounds, egg casings, starfish, sea urchins, crabs or their holes, minnows, clams, or higher life forms like sharks, leopard rays, and stingrays. A barren flat does not offer a good prognosis for bonefishing.

Rough wind can be advantageous for pursuing bonefish on the Florida flats. As long as the water temperature does not drop below the low seventies, and you can wade or boat safely to your spot, these conditions are favorable for a number of reasons. First, windy days tend to cut down on the competition by other anglers. Second, rough water cushions the sounds of your presentation landing on the water. Third, rougher waters tend to break up the water into the type of little prisms that make it harder for the fish to see the boat or wading angler with the undistorted clarity they have on ultracalm days. I like rough days when the water is basically clear because the wind has been blowing only for a day or because the water is over hard bottom and does not muddy up as when it is over marl or mud. Rough days make bonefish and other flats fish, like permit, less spooky.

The very same potent senses that help bonefish feed also help them survive. If they can see and smell what is right, they can see and smell what is wrong. Although rough days offer anglers some strategic value in easing the bonefish's ordinary wariness, conversely, calm days demand that anglers be extremely careful and delicate with their presentations. When the water surface is flat, use lighter baits, cast farther away from the fish, lead the fish, and use longer leaders with fly tackle. The high-alert powers and corresponding body structure of the bonefish enable it to enter and exit the shallowest flats with the greatest efficiency. Although redfish enter shallow waters and can be quite spooky, their small eyes and paddle tail keep them in croaker status compared to the unforgiving demands of the bonefish.

Make sure your artificial lures and flies have no off-putting scent on them, and do not taint natural live or dead baits with unnatural odors. Back in that kitchen with the delicious cooking smells—what would happen to the alluring scents of cooking conch fritters if the kitchen were filled with the smell of kerosene? Although no market researcher has interviewed any bonefish with a preference-avoidance survey for smells and tastes, you can use your imagination. Sunscreen, gas, oil, or any other potent aromatic on your baits or flies can overpower a fish's sense of smell. To test the powers of alluring smells, watch a bonefish's response to a bare fly compared to a fly with a bit of fresh shrimp smell mashed into it!

The Contrasts, Comparisons, and Uniqueness of Florida Bonefish

Although some places in the world feature miles of ankle-deep flats and vast schools of small feeding bonefish with their backs out of the water, Florida generally does not offer these conditions. Florida's oceanic bonefish move along flats that often drop off to much deeper water. Because bonefish are highly saline flats fish—unlike the brackish-loving redfish and snook—their distribution is generally toward the saltier open Atlantic Ocean or the Gulf of Mexico in the Lower Keys. This is why bonefish are more of an Atlantic-side fish on the flats of the northernmost Florida Keys. When you get down to approximately Tavernier or Upper Matecumbe Key, the ocean infuses the brackish backcountry waters with salt, so bonefish are more prevalent in these inland areas.

In the Bahamas, the feeding habits of the large schools of bonefish and the vast shallow flats conceivably allow anglers to fish and refish the same schools of fish. In Florida, you will find larger, warier bonefish with much closer access to deeper water. The vast majority of Florida bonefish will be in the Florida Keys from Key Largo to Key West, and generally in close proximity to the flats of these actual islands. With Florida bonefish, your window of opportunity to make your presentation will be narrower than in other destinations: the fish will be bigger, fewer, warier, and in my opinion, a greater challenge. If you have fished for bonefish only in the Bahamas, the Yucatan, or Christmas Island, Florida's bonefish flats will be a treat.

Florida bonefish also differ from Bahamian bonefish with respect to their feeding and movement relationships to black and red mangrove forests. In the Bahamian flats where vast fields of mangroves line the shores—like in the bights of Andros Island—fishing tactics are often planned on the falling tide because vast numbers of bonefish move into the mangroves at high tide to feed on the snails and crabs that abound among the roots. These fish are too far back in the mangroves to reach until the tide starts out; then the fish emerge like well-fattened ghosts from under the cover of the lush greenery. Although Florida's flats have mangroves too, the density and absolute size of the forests is more modest. In Florida, bonefish move into mangroves on the rising tide, but with less daily regularity and in smaller numbers. Bonefish in Florida are often found cruising the bare crowns of flats and hugging the limestone or sandy shorelines at high tide.

Florida bonefish also go mudding like Bahamian bonefish; however, fewer bonefish gather on the Florida flats, and the areas disturbed during their feeding, known as "muds," are smaller. Florida bonefish generally mud in pods and groups over soft bottom. They are tracked by following the latest smoky-looking puff of upwelling. Mudding Florida bonefish must generally be poled after and cast to in an area often less than six feet across. In the Bahamas, the muds are frequently the size of tennis courts—the guide merely anchors upwind or uptide of these huge muds, giving anglers plenty at which to cast. On the ankle-deep flats of the Marls of Abaco, the small resident bonefish are often tracked by the darkened, unearthed feeding holes that remain after their muds dissipate. In Florida, the type of bottoms, the general depths of the flats, and the large size of our bonefish make tracking by feeding holes far less common.

Bonefish Weather

Although research has identified subtypes of bonefish in Florida, the species *Albula vulpes* does not have subspecies distinctiveness as do common snook, fat snook, tarpon snook, or swordspine snook. Florida bonefish have the same preferences and characteristics as bonefish in other parts of the world. They are fairly tropical in their distribution but temperate in their environmental preferences. Unlike tarpon, which are content as long as the water is warmer than seventy-five degrees, bonefish prefer water temperatures neither too hot nor too cold, ideally from the low seventies to the mid-eighties, so you must monitor the upper and lower limits of their preferred temperature range.

Always arm yourself with a water temperature–sensing device. If you are in a skiff, your depth recorder–fish finder should have a temperature-measuring component. If you are wading, purchase the best handheld thermometer you can buy. A couple of degrees can be the difference between success and failure on the flats, because all flats species have water temperature tolerance ranges. Flats fishing without a temperature-sensing device is a self-imposed limitation that will hamper your success.

Not surprisingly, the peak times for Florida bonefish are during temperate stages of the year—specifically spring and fall. Although bonefish can be caught year-round, summer and winter carry a greater risk of the extreme temperatures and conditions that drive bonefish off the Florida flats. July ushers in the dog days of summer and flat, calm midday waters with temperatures into the nineties. Although the more tropical tarpon and permit have no problem with these conditions, bonefish simply do not like it. At this time of year, bonefishing is best in the early morning or around dusk when the water temperatures are slightly lower. When the sun is low, the overhead light is poor. You may find that fishing during the low-light ends of the day is best done around the low tides, when all you need to do is gaze at the surface for tailing and waking bonefish.

Two other situations during summer create lower water temperatures. The first situation involves the inevitable afternoon thunderstorms and showers that start inland in the Everglades and march eastward over places like Biscayne Bay. These storms often dump huge amounts of rain that can slightly cool the bay waters. This is when the days are longest, so if you let these storms rain themselves out, you may find a bit of light left in your summer day. This is a good time to fish around the low tide flats that are slightly rain-cooled and more tolerable to bonefish. If it is not low tide after a storm, pick the shallowest flat you know that will show wakes and surface bulges; poststorm summertime shallows are often totally calm.

The other summertime strategy for hot water and bonefish is to time your fishing with a strong incoming tide from the Atlantic Ocean or Gulf of Mexico. The incoming tide brings the cooler water that bonefish prefer and you can remain on the summery flats and watch the water for cruising bonefish.

Because Florida is part of the North American landmass, it is subject to seasons that include cold weather. Unlike the more constant temperatures of the South Pacific flats, you will be challenged on Florida's flats as the bonefish begin to leave the shallows with the arrival of cold fronts that plunge the water temperatures below seventy. My experience indicates that very cold water is even more intolerable to bonefish than very hot water.

You may read inspired accounts by writers and anecdotes by guides in Florida about bonefish wildly feeding in anticipation of an approaching cold front. The bottom line, however, is that bonefish do not like these weather systems. Bonefish like consistent, temperate, pleasant, stable weather.

Fishing the Florida shallows for bonefish in wintertime often requires the reverse of summertime strategies. Avoid dawn and dusk, when the water temperatures are too cool—you want to pursue deep winter bonefish during the times of day when the waters are warmest. Begin your fishing at midday and pursue the bonefish in the afternoon when the sun has had a chance to warm the waters a bit. This is a sleep-in type of fishery; moderate the gallop of your bonefish-driven glands, as it is not productive to be on the water to greet the rising sun.

Cold fronts come in different varieties of severity and duration (see chapter 5), which have varying effects on bonefish. A mild early season cold front that drops air temperatures ever so slightly and lasts only a day or two will have little effect on the water temperature. Yet because flats are shallow, they are sensitive to the influence of the air mass that sits above them. As the winter wears on and the cold fronts get colder and last longer, the shallows will inevitably start to cool. Because water temperature changes more slowly than air temperature, the flats waters of day one of a cold front will be warmer than on the following days. This gives you a chance to put on another layer of clothing and fish for bonefish a bit longer.

As you fish around the cold fronts for Florida bonefish, consider that the prevailing southeasterly tropical trade winds will go into the south and proceed clockwise into the southwest, west, northwest, and the north. How long the wind remains in those quadrants depends on the specific characteristics of each cold front. Factor the changes in wind direction, velocity, and wind chill into your bonefish and flats fishing strategies. You no longer have the luxury of the endlessly balmy days of summer. As the front passes along its track, high pressure may kick in from the east, giving rise to strong northeast winds. As things settle down and nonfront weather returns, the winds go into the east and either hold or moderate. The cycle completes itself as the wind speed drops off and returns to the southeast.

Second, generally a line of disturbed weather forms at the leading edge of the cold front, where the first wedge of rolling cold air hits Florida's prevailing warm air. That creates cloudiness, showers, and perhaps some storms. It also creates the secondary effect of changed sky conditions, which will lessen overhead light and add cloud reflections on the water. This makes it harder to see into the water to spot cruising fish, and most wintertime bonefish are cruisers, not tailers. The overhead conditions change as the front arrives, bringing clear blue skies and lots of very cold air. The return of overhead light allows you to see into the water more clearly, but now you must cope with very cold air that is sure to drop the flats temperatures within a day.

Some more reliable bonefish behaviors accompany winter and cold fronts in Florida. You can expect a shift in bonefish populations and movements more toward the Atlantic-side outside flats adjacent to the deeper and warmer ocean. My belief is that wintertime bonefish are attuned to the presence of the warming Gulf Stream offshore. You can expect to see the bonefish bunch up and run along the outside ocean flats in large schools. Some people theorize that this is for spawning purposes, while others believe the fish aggregate to generate and experience collective heat. It is possible that both conjectures are correct. Most important, these schools of fish will be feeding some of the time and can provide you with a day of excellent action.

Flats Tip: Poling Strategies for Wintertime Bonefish

Try to pole the Atlantic-side flats anywhere from Sands Cut to Tavernier in a good five to seven feet of water—because that's the depth in which the schools will be traveling. Be sure to pole in a direction whereby the sun is over your shoulder, and stay on your poling tower for optimal fish spotting in the deeper water. Be on the lookout for a large moving mass, not individual fish. As they approach, cast your bait, fly, or bucktail in front of them—you'll find out if they're feeding soon enough! If you do hook up, the school is worth fishing for. After you release your bonefish, let the school travel a good hundred yards before you fire up your engine to run around them and intercept them in their travel path once again. This is somewhat like tarpon fishing in the spring. If the school hangs around your hooked-up fish, which is rare, simply pole along judiciously toward their midst and, when you are ready, cast again.

Wintertime seems to offer more chances at large bonefish from Miami to Key West. One theory is that cold weather drives smaller bonefish off the flats, leaving the larger fish to be caught with more regularity. The other theory is that the fish are bigger because they fill up with milt or roe, as bonefish are thought to begin spawning in the winter. You can see that the winter brings some real challenges to the Florida bonefishery but also some great opportunities for adventure and rewarding catches.

A Chumming Pioneer

Chumming for bonefish had its origins with the early experiments of Captain Bill Curtis as he plied the waters of Biscayne Bay in the late 1950s. Bill was the first guide to offer poled charters on the flats of Biscayne Bay. Captain J. T. Harrod also offered bonefish charters, but he fished for bonefish out of an anchored boat. Not infrequently, Bill would encounter cold fronts, storms, high winds, or other inclement weather, which made the visibility poor for traditional poling and casting to sighted bonefish. At these times, he began to think about getting the bonefish to come to him. Armed with his knowledge of bonefish feeding habits, he staked out his boat uptide of a light sandy area. Then he cut up a handful of fresh shrimp and tossed it out in the light bottom. Before long he had some hungry bonefish in the chummed area and his clients were hooked up. In these poor conditions, the dark color of their backs created a sharp contrast over the white bottom as the bonefish came in from grassy areas to the chum.

A light sand bottom makes it easier to spot bonefish. Photo by Scott Heywood/ Angling Destinations.

Bill had discovered a viable method of attracting bonefish when conditions necessitated it.

Chumming the flats for bonefish is simple—all you need is a good downtide current or a strong wind from behind you and enough water to hold bonefish. Bonefish are perhaps the most chum-responsive species on the Florida flats. Permit also respond well to crab chum placed uptide of rock piles or on the uptide side of rubble flats. These two species are generally chummed from a stationary staked-out skiff. Sharks also "chum in" quite well.

Some guides and anglers do not like to chum for bonefish. The most intolerant anglers might even tell you that a chummed-in bonefish is a hypnotized, guaranteed-to-be-caught type of fish. Many chummed-in bonefish are simply curious window-shoppers that will not feed. You should decide for yourself what you enjoy and find effective. I find chumming for bonefish a viable, exciting method that I rely on again and again. I look forward to those moments when I stake out my skiff and wait for that ever-so-brief window of time when a bonefish bolts in to the chum, and I have perhaps five to ten seconds to make a perfect presentation or the fish is gone. It gives me the same type of electric anticipation I get when I anchor my skiff and wade very quietly up to a large tailing bonefish. Chumming for Florida bonefish is not only exciting; there are times when it seems to be the right choice. It is ideal for times on the flats when you are alone in your skiff and poling and casting to individually sighted fish is cumbersome, if not impossible. It also is a good method for pulling channel-dwelling bonefish back up to the edge of a flat during very hot or cold weather.

For optimum chumming, remain uptide and upcurrent of a white sandy patch that stands in contrast to grassy bottom. Keep the sun—whether it is cloud-muted or not—behind you and shining toward the chum area. You do not have to be in a skiff, but try to get some form of elevation. All you need is a lightweight, sure-footed stepladder with a seat or back support and you are in business. I have used this method with great success on the ocean side of Marathon during winters.

Originally I chummed by simply tossing out a handful of diced-up shrimp; however, I found that pinfish, puffers, cowfish, boxfish, stingrays, and needlefish would devour the unenclosed shrimp too quickly. The chum would not last as long as I liked, and it got fairly expensive, so I began to use a chum tube. I use a Cuban yo-yo filled with fifty feet of extremely heavy microbraid line and attach it to my chum tube. This allows me to throw and retrieve the tube quite well, and it beats tossing free chum into a headwind every time. I paint my chum tube with Day-Glo orange paint to assist me in keeping a visual fix on the tube itself and on the downtide area from which the bonefish come in.

Bonefish Tackle

Florida bonefish generally run larger than bonefish in other parts of the world. In Biscayne Bay, and even more so at Islamorada, a ten-pound bonefish is considered a trophy, but it doesn't quicken the heart rate. In these champion areas, the bonefish angler's heart starts pounding when the weights of the gray ghosts top eleven and twelve pounds, and a fifteen-pound fish is a cause for real celebration. With these parameters in mind, the six-weight fly rod or six-pound spinner that served you so well in the Marls of Abaco may prove inadequate on the flats of Florida. An eight-weight fly rod and ten-pound spinner are more realistic.

Whether you are using fly, spin, or plug tackle, your reels must be of the finest saltwater quality. Do not try to use a freshwater reel that runs the risk of seizing up. The two most important features of your reels should be an ultrasmooth drag and a line capacity of at least two hundred yards.

No discussion of bonefish or any inshore tackle is complete without a review of the microbraid line revolution. The popularity of these lines for saltwater fishing has grown exponentially for many reasons. First, microbraid has a much smaller diameter than monofilament of the same strength, so eight-pound microbraid has the diameter of two-pound mono. Thus, more microbraid line can be used on a spinning reel.

Second, because microbraid has a smaller corresponding diameter than mono, the former sinks quite well. Third, microbraids have no stretch; this translates into extremely high line sensitivity for game fish strikes and fully loaded ability to strike your bonefish.

Consider the pros and cons of using microbraid versus monofilament for bonefish. Some guides are concerned about the visibility of microbraids and the need for clear leaders, which gives spin and plug fishermen the same concerns that fly fishermen have. In addition, impossible tangles can occur when inexperienced users toss bonefish lures because they forget to hand-tighten the line on their reels periodically. Other guides feel that the increased casting distance, increased line capacity, increased sensitivity, and increased sink rate make microbraids a slam-dunk in line choice. An extensive discussion of actual line choice is beyond the scope of this book, and the choice is up to you. In my own flats fishing, I use spinning and plug tackle packed with eight-pound PowerPro microbraid line when I fish for bonefish or permit around rubble flats, rock piles, or sea fans. In these cases, I want abrasion resistance and the ability to put huge pressure on a fish in the presence of line-cutting obstacles. When I fish over sand, I relax this requirement.

Long rods simply make sense when you go bonefishing. You get a longer cast and keep more of your line out of the water when you are hooked up. Fly rods already provide good length, being around nine feet. With spinning rods, try moving to a nine-foot steelhead model and see if you feel the difference. If you love tossing small tan skimmer head jigs at bonefish with a plug rod, try increasing your rod length from the usual five and a half feet to at least six feet. It has certainly helped my tackle perform more optimally—it is possible that increasing the length of your rod when you pursue bonefish might help you, too.

Bonefish will eat live shrimp and crabs with relish. Be sure always to use the best possible hooks. My current choice is a Gamakatsu 1/0 Siwash hook. Skimmer-headed jigs with bucktail or hackle work best because of their action. Adding a small weed guard to the lure makes it even more effective. I currently use Backbone lures in very shallow water encounters over sandy or grassy bottoms. When I encounter big Florida bonefish mudding just off a flat, I use an all-white Spro bucktail jig. I find that the hookeye placement, the realistic head, and the Gamakatsu hook make this a superb jig for deeper bonefish applications. For the galaxies of fly choices, refer to books on fly fishing for bonefish.

Flats Hot Spot: Cruising Territory for Bonefish

First-time or even experienced waders who are new to South Florida will find bonefish cruising the mainland flats south of Miami's Matheson Hammock. Another good startup spot for waders is the Atlantic shoreline of Long Key State Park in the Middle Keys. Entry-level anglers with flats boats should do well in the Stiltsville area of Biscayne Bay: these flats are particularly good for bonefish when you chum the light spots on the last of the incoming tide.

Flats Tip: Big Bonefish Central

Nothing beats the shallows of Islamorada's venerable Shell Key as Big Bonefish Central. These flats are easily spotted on relevant charts on

This is the proper way to cradle a bonefish for a photo. Photo by Scott Heywood/ Angling Destinations.

the bay side of the south end of Upper Matecumbe Key. It is a short boat ride from the Overseas Highway: simply pick a day with nice weather and rising water. Bring a spinning outfit with a live shrimp and have at it!

The Big Bonefish of Islamorada, by Tim Borski

In July of 2005, I was asked by Jan Maizler to contribute to a chapter in his book, *Fishing Florida's Flats*. It was to be about bonefish, or more specifically, the actual act of bonefishing.

Florida is noted for its large bonefish. Photo by Scott Heywood/Angling Destinations.

I immediately thought of 12 or 270 other people who are better at bonefishing than I ever was or will ever be, and told him so. Maizler stuck to his guns.

So, with acknowledgment and respect to every single one of you (and you all know who you are), I'll tell what I know to be true, feel is true, and would like to believe is true . . . (heck, I'll even make some stuff up).

For all practical purposes, this section deals with large bonefish. I mean fish easily exceeding ten pounds; a real ten pounds, not that "other" ten that so many toss around. And, although I have never caught a bone on fly over thirteen pounds, two ounces, I have been fortunate enough to fish with very talented friends and anglers who have bested them on fly to fourteen pounds, eight ounces—a very real fourteen-eight, mind you.

The way I see it is, you, as the angler, are obligated to do some homework. Pick the biggest tides of the month and fish hard all day. Begin with tails, end with tails. Mudders fill the sunlight hours. It is an incredibly rewarding fishery, yet wonderfully boring if you're not

Bonefish in a mangrove. Pen and ink drawing by Tim Borski.

hooked up, which by the way, can be days on end. But then again, you're looking for a "Booner": a Boone and Crockett–class record-book fish.

While fishing giants in Islamorada, my neck of the woods, if you're not deep into your backing by 7:00 a.m., you may as well head to the Dead Animal, Lorelei, or OV . . . shoot, maybe even Woody's. Have a cheap pizza for breakfast, knock back a few cold ones, and climb into the saddle again. Ya got all day, don'tcha?

This is bonefishing, Islamorada style, "two yards and a cloud of mud," baby. Sunlight is your friend. By 10:00 a.m. you will have forgotten all about the morning, the incredible sunrise over the highway, blown shots at tough fish, and the bonnethead that took your last TK Special, and you'll probably be wondering why your hair smells like ciggy-butt smoke and your lap . . . well, whatever. Suck it up. Pull out the nine-weight and the bug with the heavy lead eyes. There is work to be done.

These are the big leagues. Good fun. Bright skies and bright muds are a pretty good recipe for success.

First and foremost, in order to catch 'em, ya gotta fish where they live. As a direct result of the Bonefish and Tarpon Unlimited tagging studies, we now know the little buggers move around quite a bit; however, some areas are frequented more consistently than others, and on top of that, it is very possible there are broad areas that a few big, stubborn homebodies seldom vacate.

In Islamorada, where I live, my choices, geographically speaking, are relatively simple.

Begin on the bay side of Tavernier Creek. A chart will show you Cross Bank. Head north and westish to Crane Key and then East Key. Dip southwest along the narrow bank that will dump you off at West and Crab keys. Turn south and follow Ironwood Bank until you get to Shell Key. Shell is the center (but not necessarily the best place) of the universe. From there, southwest will take you to the plainly visible Lignum Vitae Key. Just past this island are Peterson Key Bank and the infamous swash. Once there, follow the well-marked channel toward the Overseas Highway and have lunch at the Hungry Tarpon adjacent to Robbie's. For a couple or three bucks, buy a bucket of stinky stuff and feed the large gray fish off their dock.

Proceed northeast along the highway, and pass Papa Joes. (You have already been there today, right?) Swerve past the world-renowned Lorelei and watch the markers as you head back toward Tavernier Creek. This will put you in very dangerous water if you are stubborn enough to insist on giant bones.

Sure, the real trophies get into other surrounding waters through osmosis, but you will most assuredly die slowly and alone if you choose to wait them out. I feel the places on the periphery of the "big oval" are sorta like bluegrass music . . . they're great when they happen, but not the place you want to get to early in the morning and wait for the band to show up.

Now that we have our geographical bearings, let me take ya for a ride. We will cover some good stuff on big bones, try to be normal, pretend nobody was looking, and then get on with our lives.

The Fishery at a Glance

Most anglers, but by a small margin, use spinning gear. This is closely linked to seasonal changes and tournament formats. The anglers who opt for spinning gear do so for simple reasons. The fish are ridiculously tough, the wind seems to blow incessantly during the prime seasons, and the live bait used gives one an edge when it is all hitting the fan too quickly. Also, when over the course of a long, long day, your one and only shot may very well be the difference between a good conversation with Joe at Uncle's or just ordering from the bar and telling anyone who will listen, "It was slow."

Spinning gear and a fresh crab will make most dinner conversations more fun. Speaking of which, the fresh stuff helps. Shrimp are probably the most frequently used offerings; however, crabs have a big following, too. It seems just when you think the crabs will work best because the fish are wise to shrimp, you'll get a couple of clean refusals on them, only to have a Mongo Bozo turn herself inside out to pile onto a couple of skimpy shrimp threaded up the line. Go figure.

In any case, both are readily available and affordable most times, so it pays to stock up on each. The waters of spring and fall are cool enough that they'll stay alive overnight. You're fishing again tomorrow, aren't ya?

Secret Number One

> When a fish bites a crab or shrimp, point your rod tip directly at it
> and begin to reel a million times the speed of light times a trillion.
>
> CAPTAIN MARK

It is just before daybreak and you have six crabs and a dozen choice shrimp. This will last you until morning decides to break into day—the transition that lasts an hour or two while the sun climbs, giving light. Go in, have the breakfast of your choice, and sally forth as the light gets good.

If you choose to begin with the crab, string a lively male on a good sharp hook while keeping your trusty pliers close at hand. Most times, what will happen is you will be alerted early by either tipping or tailing, and by movement and mudding after breakfast.

The standard procedure is to grab the crab in your left hand, pliers in right, and gently crush the critter's shell. Pitching upcurrent of your target should result in the current sweeping the fresh scent to the fish before she changes course. If your math is correct on the intercept, the result will be both beautiful and "field trialesque."

The sight of a whopper bone, bird-dogging back and forth across the current looking for the crab you just placed, is one of life's great treasures. Watch as she gets a snoot full, pulls up, and then piles on. Boink! Big point, big tail. In a second, she is off and running and running. Remember, point your rod toward your target and reel a million times the speed of light, times—you know!

Fall

The "girls of fall" may not be full of eggs, but—and this is a huge but—a fat bonefish in the "oval" that has been feeding hard due to cooling, more friendly water temps, and the shortening of daylight hours, will be a fighter. She will slide downhill deep into your backing every single time. If you couple this with a better release ratio due to friendlier water temps, you will find a win-win situation.

The Fly Rod

Almost as many folks down this way choose the fly rod as their weapon of choice; however, the best tend to master spin and fly. They use whichever one suits their fancy on any given day. Should you choose this route, you will need quality equipment.

Quality reels abound, as do rods. This will be completely your choice and one that can, many times, be made easier by visiting a local fly shop or three. Don't, however, spend so much time that it all becomes confusing.

Personally, I get up in the morning, have a big cup of cold coffee, and pick a rod-and-reel outfit off my rack that has the line I choose to use for the day. I make sure the line is either brand new or really clean. Simple as that.

I have many rods and many reels. It's my fly lines, in most cases, that keep me from looking like a goofball.

I build a leader the night before or simply add a butt section in the morning, depending on the day's prospects. Normally, I start with a fairly long five- or six-foot butt section of forty-pound, four feet of twenty-five, and two feet of sixteen or twelve. Feel free to tweak as the day goes on and, if you are so inclined, learning to tie a quick, neat knot will help more than I can say. All my leaders are fluorocarbon—the whole length—no exceptions.

A lot of this fishery is played out in fairly deep water, which in effect gives the fish a large "living room." It makes sense to use huge flies and fairly aggressive approaches. If you think about it, a large window of awareness promotes ease. Imagine you are in a closet and someone sets a sparrow loose. Of course, you will flinch because your world is very small, and you think "bat" or "spider" or worse.

Now, stand in an auditorium. The same sparrow is going to have you look up and point at it. You will probably even say, "Hey, look at the stupid sparrow!" You will be able to do that because it didn't scare you. Your immediate world is much larger. Follow me?

Flies

Let's talk about flies for the elders.

First and foremost, these bugs tend to be bigger than late-season grasshoppers, but slightly smaller than full-grown tiger salamanders. They make much better bass food in most locales than they would ever make bonefish food elsewhere. But then we are talking about Islamorada, not most bone destinations.

I am of the impression that even though there are areas where the fish can be as big—shoot, maybe sometimes bigger—I think the need for big flies in Islamorada is twofold. Our fish, on average, forage for larger prey. This, combined with the larger than average fish, means a substantial hook is needed to keep stuck to them once they are out a hundred yards or so. It is damned tough to get a small fly to behave well enough on a big hook to fool an old fish.

Also, all my flies have weed guards. It is easy to push them down if you don't need them, but with a little common sense, they will not interfere with hook sets and keeping fish stuck. Quick rule of thumb: twelve-pound hard mono on #4s and lightly weighted #2s; sixteen-pound Mason hard mono on #1s and heavily weighted flies. You should choose between double and single.

Poling Strategies

I have no poling strategies beyond the extreme right (tricking someone into doing it for you) or the far left (pick an edge and follow it); sooner or later they'll find you . . . or not. Remember, if a particular fringe isn't responding, cross the channel and ride the other side. This is real good advice in a real hard game. Also, try not to find yourself up on the top of the flats too often. The fish you are looking for live on the contours.

Dirt roads, second growth, and channel edges have always spelled fun for me.

There ya go, Jan. I muddled through it, gave you some good advice, and didn't even have to make anything up. The rest is up to the patience and perseverance of the readers.

One last piece of advice: One night, many years ago, outside at the Lorelei Cabana Bar, I overheard Captain Billy Knowles talking to someone and he said: "Son, ya gotta find current. No current, no bones." These words have echoed in my head and saved me a thousand times over the last dozen years or so.

Thanks, Captain Bill. (And, of course, sorry for eavesdropping.)

Good night and good fishin'.

Tarpon

With Captain Greg Poland
and Captain Mike Locklear

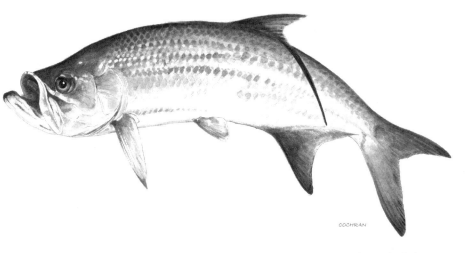

Illustration by Vaughn Cochran

Tarpon (*Megalops atlanticus*)
Size Range: 2 to 243 pounds
Florida State Record: 243 pounds
Florida Habitat: Passes, cuts, beaches, canals, saltwater and brackish flats
   of Florida
Baits: Live shrimp, crabs, pinfish, mullet, bucktail jigs, plugs, and flies
Tackle: 12- to 15-pound spinning or baitcasting; 11- to 12-weight fly
Tarpon Hot Spots: Monster-sized tarpon over 150 pounds invade the flats
   off Homosassa, north of Tampa, usually in May.

Tarpon in the Florida Keys and Backcountry, by Captain Greg Poland

In the Islamorada area we are fortunate to have the backcountry, which is the Gulf side and the Everglades National Park. And we have the ocean side and the bridges—all excellent tarpon hunting grounds. A push of tarpon comes down the east coast from the Miami downtown area and Government Cut, feeding all winter on the baitfish. Then a spring push and migration occurs, when those fish head down toward Elliot Key and Biscayne Bay, then to the Ocean Reef and Key Largo area, and after that, they head all the way down the Florida Keys. The tremendous number of bridges around Islamorada creates another staging area where those fish can get from the Atlantic Ocean into the Gulf of Mexico and lie around.

Keep in mind that certain groups of tarpon are migratory, while others are resident fish.

Tarpon Habitat

In our area, small resident tarpon are born around mangroves and hang out there. Many of these fish grow up to be in the twenty-five- to thirty-pound range. I am sure some very old, big fish live in the area and do not migrate. Most of the migratory tarpon I see on the beautiful crystal clear ocean flats are, on average, between forty-five and fifty-pound "ocean fish," and they may go all the way up to seventy-five pounds. These are migratory fish that you encounter on the flats in the springtime.

Pursuing these migratory fish on the ocean side of Islamorada is generally done with a pushpole or an electric motor. The standard operating procedure is that someone is pushing the boat from an elevated platform over the engine, and someone is standing on the bow. I generally like to have one angler on the bow and to place a second angler, when there is one, on the center console, simply watching the action. In the season from midwinter to May, the fish will be heading toward Key West; we call these tarpon "southbounders." Then the same fish will be heading in the opposite direction from approximately mid-May through July. Every day fish come out from the backcountry around a bridge near downtown Islamorada. They start swimming toward Miami—as singles or doubles or a string of fish—and they run into a group of eight or ten tarpon. I think they jump right into the middle and start swimming to wherever the mass is going. These fish are always on the move, and it is difficult to determine the size of the group or the weight of each individual fish: it is a truly exciting fishery with a high element of the unexpected.

Tarpon Spotting Tactics on the Flats

For ocean tarpon fishing in the morning, we like to go out at about ten o'clock: that is when you have the light. If it is very calm and the tarpon are rolling, you can go out earlier, but generally, between seven and ten o'clock you cannot see the fish swimming. This is especially so early in the season, because you are looking into the sun. Later in the season, you have the opposite: the sun is behind you, and the fish are traveling from Key West to Miami, so it is easy to see the fish over a white hole. I like to put the boat on a grass patch while looking at a white spot in front of the bow. I do not think that tarpon deliberately swim over the lighter areas, but I have been successful utilizing these high visibility spots and being in the right place at the right time.

I start my day knowing the stage of the tide. If it is a low tide, I work farther out toward the ocean because I want to stay in about three to six feet of water. That range of depth is large. When I start my day, I look for that first fish or that first school of fish. If the first fish is in four and a half feet of water, then I try to stay in about four and a half feet of water. I pole around and see if I can find more tarpon moving in that zone. This is harder to do in the early morning with low light. If I am poling around at ten o'clock in the morning when I can see, it is easier to determine that the fish may be twenty-five feet out in, say, six feet of water. So I simply move out to six feet of water. I always start my day that way—poling.

But if I go out on a rainy morning and the water is rough, I might go to a specific spot that I know in the area. For instance, if I were looking down a straight shoreline and there were some rocks sticking out on a low tide, I would know that the fish would have to swim around them, so I would go to that feature, which we like to call a "point." I might anchor the boat out or stake the boat out if the ground will allow it. Generally, when a tarpon swims around a point it makes some sort of unusual movement. It might roll, and then you can see it! You should always be looking for some sort of a clue.

Tarpon "Chasing" and Hunting Tactics

Personally, I don't like electric motors. I find they scare the tarpon. A lot of anglers chase the fish down with electric motors and constantly cast after the fish but are never optimally successful. If a group of fish comes by and no one else is fishing, I prefer to let the fish go on three or four hundred feet past me. Then I start the boat and idle out to twelve feet of water. I might run half a mile down and set up again in six feet of water and pole, trying to let the fish come to the boat instead of my chasing them down. You always want to be ahead of the fish and know where the fish are before you start casting, whether you're using bait or fly.

Another effective way to chase tarpon begins in your own house through the study of probable tarpon habitat. If you are planning to fish the Islamorada area and are renting a skiff locally to pursue tarpon, buy a satellite chart at one of the local shops. Look down the coast, try to find an area that looks shallow, and let that be your starting point. If you are hunting tarpon early in the season, start on the Key West side of a point. Chasing or hunting down tarpon is a skill that comes through the investment of time and effort.

If you are coming to Florida in pursuit of your tarpon dream, hiring a fishing guide is an excellent investment. Chances are you only have a couple of days to spare and you want to make the most of your tarpon fishing time. If you have a little more time, you may want to experiment on your own in a rental skiff, but a guide is always a worthwhile investment because a guide is a teacher. As a young man, I used to save my money to go out with some of the guides who have contributed to this book and some others who have taught me along the way. I find I am still learning from some of them.

Tarpon habitats range from the salty ocean all the way into brackish and then fresh water, so your hunt for the tarpon can take you into many different zones. The main reason I moved to Islamorada in the Florida Keys is because it has so many diverse locations to fish for tarpon on the flats. You can fish on the ocean flats, in the backcountry, or in the Everglades. I might fish the laid-up tarpon in the backcountry shallows and then go very deep into the Everglades to brackish or sometimes even fresh water. Often I fish so far into the Everglades that I see—and catch—tarpon along with black bass, so there is definitely fresh water there. Snook and other game fish also inhabit that area. A tarpon can live just about anywhere. You can find them deep in the Everglades in dirty, mucky water. You can find them in gin-clear water in the ocean. And if you look hard enough, you might find tarpon under most fillet tables in the Florida Keys.

Tarpon are opportunistic feeders. Sometimes a summer day's onshore breeze stacks seaweed toward the shoreline of our oceanside flats. Always check out these areas despite their unpleasant smell and appearance. I have often found tarpon feeding on the shrimp and crabs inside those weeds. This does not occur with just an occasional clump, but rather with a growing raft of weeds with enough crustaceans to make it worthwhile for the tarpon to feed along its borders.

A Tarpon Hot Spot: The "Worm Run"

The annual palolo worm runs create tarpon events on the summer flats. The palolo is a very small worm that pops out of the coral in countless numbers, and thousands of aroused tarpon mass for this event. You would think that all these tarpon would just crash out of the water to eat the worm. Often the silver king just swims up and sips the worm in: it is so delicate to see a hundred-pound fish do this. The palolo worm looks like a two-inch night crawler. The worm run is quite an amazing event that occurs off of Long Key in the Islamorada area. Another worm run—probably the most popular one—occurs off Bahia Honda Key, which is about thirty miles short of Key West, and another one occurs at Key West. Timing of the worm run is one of the most difficult things in nature to predict. If you were to go every day from afternoon to night in May and June, you might get lucky enough to find it. If you did, you would have a truly exciting shallow water inshore adventure.

Generally, the late afternoon during an outgoing tide is when the worm run occurs. A lot of the fishing guides get together and talk about it: did it "go off" today, or will it go off tomorrow? One possible clue is that a few days before the hatch, the tarpon get finicky and refuse to strike our lures and flies—especially the ocean-run tarpon.

At these times, you just sense that something is going to happen, especially when the full moon and the outgoing tide converge during the last ten days of May. Being in the right place at the right time for the worm run is not a precise science—this year I went to Bahia Honda three times and later learned that it happened in Islamorada. I drove right past it!

"Laid-Up" Tarpon

Tarpon are generally quite comfortable in Florida flats waters of three- to six-foot depths. Unlike bonefish, which are almost always moving and grazing on the flats bottom, tarpon love to vary their flats behavior in this water column. Sometimes they seem to rest and float perfectly still. We often see this in the Florida Keys backcountry, and we refer to these stationary fish as "laid-up" tarpon. You might be poling a Florida Bay backcountry flat on a calm morning and encounter a ninety-pound fish hovering in fairly murky water. It will generally be visible because it is very calm and the fish is floating close to the surface, sometimes even letting its tail and dorsal fin protrude out of the water. These fins look a bit like sticks as you pole up.

Fishing for laid-up tarpon in the backcountry is my favorite type of fishing for the silver king. It is the ultimate stealth game—you must quietly pole over to the fish in total calmness, knowing that any sound will spook it. Using a fly rod, you try to throw the fly far enough from the fish not to spook it but close enough for your quarry to see the fly and strike. I like to use a five-foot lead in front of the fish, and very slowly twitch it. If you see the tail kick, the next thing you should see is an awesome big silver flash as the tarpon gobbles your presentation. Your flat, calm, beautiful surroundings, quiet as everything was, yield to pandemonium.

Tarpon Tackle

When sight casting and poling for ocean-running fish, I usually use a seven-foot spinning rod—a graphite rod with a medium-sized tip. And I use a line of fifteen-pound breaking strength because I will be throwing a live crab, a soft-bodied artificial, or a weighted fly. Fifteen-pound line can cast fairly well but gives you the power you need to put the pressure on a fish that tops one hundred pounds.

It's easy to see that the tarpon's armored mouth makes it a hard fish to hook. Photo by Scott Heywood/Angling Destinations.

My favorite way of spin fishing for the ocean-running tarpon out on the flats is the following: I use a live crab about the size of a half dollar, or maybe slightly larger than that; you can buy these at any of the bait shops. Hook the crab in the "corner" of the shell with a 2/0 hook, and perhaps add a split shot, which is just a very small weight, to increase your casting distance and sink rate. I use a sixty-pound fluorocarbon leader of maybe five or six feet long, tied to a doubled monofilament or microbraid line. Although tarpon do not have teeth, newcomers to Florida's flats need to realize the silver king has a very rough mouth—much like fifty-grit sandpaper—that can chafe through lighter leader material quite easily.

The superbraided lines cast better than monofilament. It's important to point out that for the same breaking strength of line, the superbraids have a much smaller diameter than monofilament. In addition, and in contrast to monofilament, the superbraids do not stretch: if you strike the fish by pulling up your rod for twelve inches, that hook is going to move for twelve inches.

On the business end of my tackle, I like the fluorocarbon because it sinks faster than mono and is virtually invisible. If I am going to

This is an effective way to hold a small, tired tarpon for unhooking. Photo by Scott Heywood/Angling Destinations.

cast live bait, I use a live crab. If the weather is suboptimal with poor sighting conditions, I might anchor or stake out my skiff and put a live mullet out of the back of the boat; you can buy these at a tackle shop or collect them with a cast net. I put the mullet "on a cork," meaning what we call tarpon corks in the Keys. These items are about the size of a tennis ball. You rig it above your leader on the same spinning tackle. Hook the mullet right in the lip, cast it off the back of the boat, and let it swim around. Meanwhile, I have a customer in the front of the boat with the live crab.

Sometimes you cannot stake out your skiff with your pushpole because the bottom is too hard. Although many Florida flats anglers rely on the new electric stern-mounted anchoring poles, I use the traditional anchoring method when I am trying to keep my boat stationary for long periods of time. I use a regular Danforth-style anchor with a six-foot chain, fifty feet of anchor line, and at the very end—five feet up from there—I have a red buoy and a clip. If we hook a fish, we just unclip the anchor, leave it there with the buoy, and run off and fight the fish. Most important, I find that the anchor line doesn't deter the fish from swimming right by the boat.

I do not make a practice of casting finfish baits at tarpon on the flats. My strategy when fishing with a live, swimming bait, such as pinfish or mullet, is to present the bait swimming around on its own and hope that a tarpon finds it. If I throw a crab at a sighted tarpon, I generally lead the fish ten feet. Sometimes I throw it with the cork, and sometimes without. I experiment a little to find out which presentation is drawing more strikes.

Regarding bait casting tackle, although I guide 230 to 250 days per year and I own three wonderful baitcasting rods and reels, I have not handed one to a customer in seven or eight years. It's just not something that's done anymore. Baitcasting or plug casting tackle is more frequently used for the baby tarpon, or by the experienced angler snook fishing in the Everglades. This tackle was popular in the old days as illustrated by some of the old fishing tournament photos, but it's something that everybody has gotten away from. Approximately half of the anglers in the Florida Keys are fly fishing, and the rest are spin fishing these days. One of the reasons baitcasting may be less popular is that if you are throwing into a headwind and get a backlash, it would be hard to recast quickly to the tarpon passing by your skiff. Generally, with a fly rod, as long as your line is clear on the deck, it's not all that hard, provided you have the proper presentation.

When fly fishing for tarpon under fifty pounds, I recommend a ten-weight fly rod. Most fly rods are nine feet long; some may be inches shorter or longer. Go to a fly shop and find the one that fits you best. For the ocean-going fish in the forty- to seventy-pound range, I tend to go up to the next size. I find that the ten-, the eleven-, and the twelve-weights, although very similar, are also very different. I like an eleven-weight myself—as do a lot of my anglers—for ocean-going tarpon. I recommend the twelve-weight fly rod for the largest tarpon. If you are only going to have one fly rod, I recommend an eleven-weight. If you are going to get two outfits, then I recommend a ten-weight and a twelve-weight. Like a golfer with a whole bag of clubs, choose the best rod for the situation.

Different fly lines—floating lines, sinking lines, a floating line with a sinking tip—are made for different situations. When I fish for ocean-run tarpon, I use a floating line in the morning and a "sink tip" for the rest of the day. If I am fishing in the backcountry for laid-up tarpon, I start with a floating line. If there are a lot of weeds around, I use a sink-tip: it brings the fly just under the surface, so it does not snag on anything as I cast.

On a fly reel, start with about two hundred yards of backing, which is the material that's your last hope in regaining the fish. The backing is the first thing that goes onto the reel. Then add a fly line that is either 90 or 110 and ten feet. Choose the mono tip, the floating line, or the sinking line, depending on the conditions. Then add what's called a butt section: about a four- or five-foot piece of fifty-pound mono or fluorocarbon. I prefer fluorocarbon because it is invisible and it sinks better. When rigging the business end, I generally start with a piece of fifty-pound fluorocarbon attached to a piece of thirty-pound fluorocarbon. The next part of the leader construction is the tippet, which is the lightest part of all and therefore determines the breaking strength of your entire fly rod outfit. If this light section of line is sixteen pounds breaking strength and you catch a hundred-pound tarpon on this outfit, you'll typically say that you caught the fish on a sixteen-pound tippet.

Use a piece of sixteen-pound tippet that is about seventeen inches long. The final component of the leader construction is the bite tippet, which is the piece of the leader that will come in contact with the fish's mouth. The pound test, diameter, and finish of the bite tippet are determined by the roughness and possible teeth of the target game fish. The bite tippet, including the knots, cannot be over twelve inches long. For tarpon, start with a sixty-pound fluorocarbon bite tippet, and then attach the fly. This entire length that runs from the fly line to the fly cannot be over fifteen feet in tournament situations. Therefore, you can strategize that when you are out there fishing and a tarpon is approaching, you are going to lead it by ten feet and you have twenty-five feet of clear line before you get to any fish-spooking line coloration. All you want your tarpon to encounter is a realistic, alluring fly that seems to be unattached to anything. Your goal is leader "invisibility."

Fighting Tactics for Tarpon

The tarpon, in my opinion, is a great gamester. I think of the action as a sort of ballet that turns into rugby. What I mean is that everything is very quiet, and the motor is off, and the place is perfectly serene, and all of a sudden your guide spots this fish. The tarpon is swimming down the bank at you and is probably four to seven feet long and weighs somewhere between 50 and 150 pounds, and it might have fifteen friends along. All of a sudden things turn to mayhem. Whether you are bait fishing or fly fishing, you put your offering out there, and if you are lucky, the fish comes up and grabs it. And when the fish grabs it, you look into this upturned mouth that all the old-timers call the "bucket mouth." And whether it is a crab the size of a half dollar or a fly that is four inches long, it just disappears into this hole.

When you are bait fishing with a spinning outfit and the fish closes its mouth and you reel as fast as you can until you feel the weight on the other end—that's the fish. Then you reel just a little more, and then you strike to your right or your left, whichever hand you favor, and no higher than your shoulders. When you are using a braided line, the length of the strike is going to be as far as you pull the rod—that is the way the hook is going to move. When you strike a tarpon on a spinning reel, whether you are using a circle hook or a J hook, point the rod at the fish and reel. With a circle hook, do not strike—just reel until the fish starts swimming away and then put a slight bow into the rod. With a J hook, reel until you feel the weight of the fish, and then strike, and then reel again.

Usually, just a few seconds later, that fish is going to start running away, and most of the time it is going to jump out of the water—sometimes clearing the water totally. If it is a very big fish, it may only clear the water halfway. When it jumps, you have to "bow" to the silver king by pointing the rod at the leaping tarpon to give some slack line. When a fish that weighs as much as a hundred pounds jumps out of the water, the water no longer compensates for its huge weight. In addition, the jumping tarpon is trying to dislodge that bait by violently shaking its head back and forth, perhaps three feet one way and then the other. When you bow to the tarpon—by giving it the extra line— you are attempting to prevent broken lines, chafed-through leaders, and pulled hooks. When the tarpon lands back in the water, reel up that slack and go right back into a bent-rod position. When the tarpon is running, you want to let that spinning reel's drag work. As your spinning line is going out against the drag on the reel, it is going backward on the spool; therefore, you never want to crank against the running drag, because that spins the line itself and creates line twist.

Basic Fly Casting for Tarpon

Most newcomers to fly tackle do not realize that the setup in fly tackle is fairly simple. It includes the backing, the fly line, the constructed leader, and the fly itself. When you use fly tackle to pursue tarpon, there's really no need to be able to cast a hundred feet: although many anglers can cast that far, the truth is that, on average, the fish is going to be caught about thirty feet away from the boat. There is a fantastic place in Islamorada called Buchanan Bank. It is the old-school place to go tarpon fishing because the skiffs are staked out in the classic orderly, lineal fashion. The skiffs thus do not interfere with one another as the tarpon come out of a basin and swim down into a pocket; then they swim out past the boats. On a day of tarpon fishing there may be five or more boats staked out. I have been in the third or fourth boat and caught a tarpon. It is perfect for a beginner angler because you can see the fish coming. Someone in the boat in front of you will shout, "Three coming," or something like that, and you have an eleven o'clock shot. What I mean by that is that the bow of the boat is twelve o'clock. To your right is one o'clock and to your left is eleven o'clock. You have to cast about thirty or thirty-five feet to reach the cruising tarpon. Your goal is to lay that fly line right out in front of the fish, aiming to lead him by ten or fifteen feet, and then you make a strip. Sometimes you make small little strips.

A strip means retrieving the fly line through your rod by hand, and the idea is to have the fly line fall in an orderly fashion at your feet. For instance, if you are a right-handed caster, you hold the rod in your right hand and lay the line out thirty feet. With your left hand you grab the line, and you retrieve your fly by pulling the line back to the boat with your left hand—in approximately one-foot increments—through the curled index finger of your right hand, which is holding the rod. As the fish comes up and eats the fly, you get a good hold of the rod cork with your right hand and sharply "strip-strike" by pulling the fly line back toward your body with your left hand.

Try to take up line to sink your hook, well sharpened, I hope, into its mouth. As the tarpon turns away after striking, your goal is to have the fly get caught and stuck in the corner of the fish's mouth. As the tarpon runs off and jumps, your goal is to keep that hook well sunk in that very same spot.

As you strip-strike—and feel the pressure or the weight of the fish on the rod—you sweep the rod sharply to the right, which is striking the fish with the rod, just as you would with a spinner. In essence, you are learning to strike the fish in two ways concurrently with fly tackle.

Then there is only one more step to perform. As you recall, your fly line is piled on the deck below you in an "orderly" fashion. The fly line needs to be piled well enough below you so that it can be pulled back outward through the rod guides by the hooked fish without fouling on the rod guides or the reel. This is known as "clearing" the line. If that process goes well, you will have a direct connect between the running fish, the bent rod, and the taut line on the reel. This is known as getting your fish "on the reel."

Nothing about fly fishing is mystical or scary. What is important for the novice fly fisherman to realize is that while there's plenty of room for growth, it is not hard to catch a nice tarpon on a fly rod after some simple instruction. If you come down and book two days with a guide, your first half of your first day will probably be devoted to instruction and teaching. If you have never used fly tackle before, you can be comfortably casting thirty-five feet within a half a day; by the second half of the day you can be fishing. On the second day, you will be thoroughly enjoying yourself. Fly fishing is just like using any other tackle type: after the mastery of some basic techniques, you are ready to do battle with the silver king.

Best Times of the Year for Tarpon in the Florida Keys

Because Islamorada features the Everglades, the ocean, and the back-country, we can fish for a lot more of the year than in other places in

Florida. The early season for the backcountry and the Everglades area is in March. I would not recommend tarpon fishing in the Islamorada area before March because the water on the flats is a little too cool. Flats anglers seeking tarpon should realize that each of these areas in Florida features different habitats and populations of fish with differing onsets of tarpon season. Therefore, it is best to check with guides, tackle shops, and outdoor writers to get a seasonal fix on your destination.

Tarpon like warm water temperatures. To me, the best fishing of all is when we get warm weather in March, because everybody is planning their tarpon vacation for May, and here you are all alone with all the silver kings. The greater part of the season when those conditions could be achieved might be as late as March through October; however, our "core" tarpon fishing season is about March through August. The prime time for the oceanside tarpon is the last week of April to the first week of July. As with anything else in fishing, it can go either way, with an early or a late season.

Tarpon Weather

Amid the Gulf Stream, the Straits of Florida, and the Gulf of Mexico, Florida is positioned in the migratory path of *Megalops atlanticus*. Studies have shown that tarpon previously caught across the Gulf of Mexico in Louisiana and perhaps as far away as Mexico have been caught off Florida's west coast.

Three groups of tarpon are relevant to Florida, and each group responds differently to the state's changing weather. The residential smaller "grass" tarpon of the Gold Coast rivers and the residential larger tarpon of the Gold Coast cuts are able to overwinter in South Florida by living in the comparative warmth of deep inland rivers or ocean cuts and feeding on the indigenous shrimp, crabs, and finfish.

Large schools of tarpon invade Florida's flats and shallows in late spring when the marine waters reach seventy-five degrees. These can generally be considered migratory tarpon. The first flats they may begin traveling across are around Homosassa, the beachfront flats surrounding Boca Grande, Nine Mile Bank in Florida Bay, and the oceanside flats from Elliot Key down to Big Pine Key. If April is warm and yields seventy-five degree water, the fish may move onto the flats early. Every good flats fisherman is a hunter—watch the weather closely!

Flats Tip: Bow to the Silver King

When a tarpon goes up in the air and shakes its head, in order to prevent it from shooting the hook or the lure right back at you on a spinning rod, bow to that tarpon to increase the chances of keeping the hook lodged in its mouth. As soon as the fish starts to move again, put maximum pressure back on it. In the midst of the battle, if the tarpon's tail is not "kicking," keep pulling the fish back toward the boat. If its tail is kicking, simply keep pressure on the fish.

As the battle goes on, the tarpon may come up and take a breath of air as if to rejuvenate itself, like when you take a gulp of Gatorade. While it is up having a breath of air, do what we call the "down and dirty." Put the rod upside down and pull backward as if you were leading a dog on a leash—right down its back. Do not be concerned that the line is going to wrap around the fish. Just pull right down its back because that slows it down. Try to continue these tactics until your prize is alongside the boat and ready for release. If the fish is weak after you unhook it, move it back and forth in the water to reoxygenate the gills until the prize is thoroughly rehabilitated. Then gently release the fish to swim away and continue its magical life.

Flats Hot Spots: Tarpon Mecca in the Keys

The shallows from Rodriguez Key down to Duck Key are an ocean tarpon fishing Mecca for me! On the bay side lies Florida Bay, which is an entirely different world. No beginner should try to fish this area because it is unmarked for navigation and therefore is potentially dangerous. You can run aground. The oceanside waters are clean, and if you are careful you are not going to hurt yourself. I do not recommend fishing in the backcountry without a guide.

Although tarpon are all over the shallow ocean from Elliot Key to Key West, a real hot spot is Rodriguez Key, which is on the south end of Key Largo. You can find this key on a chart. This island has a large flat that forms a bank from the mangrove island out approximately a

The tarpon's large eye gives it the piercing vision to see and grab flies and lures immediately. Photo by Scott Heywood/Angling Destinations.

hundred yards, creating a big white strip. It is a great place for a beginner to go, stake out the boat, and watch for the tarpon to come down. If you see a fishing guide in a boat, I suggest you give him a couple of hundred yards of room as a courtesy. Stay away from human waterborne activity such as personal watercraft.

Flats Tip: Poling Oceanside Flats for Tarpon

On a calm early summer day, carefully run your skiff to the oceanside flats of Long Key Point south of Islamorada or Elliot Key east of Biscayne Bay. In either area, the drill is the same: approach from the deeper ocean waters and pole your skiff into six feet of water. Keep the poling track of your skiff roughly parallel to the shoreline. At dawn or early in the morning, look for rolling fish that you can intercept. As the sun gets higher, look for groups of cruising tarpon that are visible in the water column.

A Land of Giant Tarpon

No book on Florida flats fishing would be complete without a section on fishing the shallows for Homosassa's giant tarpon. I was fortunate that Captain Mike Locklear, one of that area's premier tarpon guides, agreed to share his abundant knowledge of the silver king. He spoke and I listened. Captain Mike took care of the paints, palette, and scenery, while I did what I could to help us word-paint a small yet accurate portrait of this wondrous and competitive Florida fishery.

The Legendary Tarpon of Homosassa, by Captain Mike Locklear

It is early May and for weeks a mass of giant tarpon have been swimming across the Gulf of Mexico en route to Homosassa, sixty miles north of Tampa on Florida's west coast. The actual starting point of their migration is a mystery.

Although May 1 is the official beginning of Homosassa tarpon season, some anglers come earlier to get a shot at a really big fish—the theory is that the tarpon are more apt to eat the fly when little or no fishing pressure has occurred. Generally, the big tarpon reach their greatest numbers during the first three weeks of May, provided that the water temperature climbs to seventy-six degrees. While June is a great month to catch a smaller tarpon between seventy and a hundred and forty pounds, some regulars have extended the season past June into early July.

As the fish arrive, the guides and their anglers stand ready to do battle after many hours of preparing their tackle and equipment. The giant tarpon—some topping two hundred pounds—and the anglers will meet on the gin-clear flats off Homosassa.

Gentlemen, Choose Your Weapons!

Flies were the creative preoccupation of the guides and anglers as they waited through the long, cold winter for the arrival of the Homosassa giants. Some of the aficionados would tie up as many as thirty or forty flies. Although colors in every shade have caught these monsters,

You might have to get in the water to achieve this ideal tarpon pose. Photo by Scott Heywood/Angling Destinations.

Fishing for trophy tarpon demands the finest fly reels. Photo by Bass Pro Shops.

color combinations favored by the experts consist of orange, yellow, red, green, blue, black, brown, and white. Some fly constructions are of the bunny strip type, while others are made of Puglisi materials. One old favorite pattern is a splayed fly with three feathers on each side, a collar, and an epoxy head with a red eye on each side.

The weapon within your fly should be a very strong and highly sharpened 5/0 saltwater hook. Give thought to using a slightly offset hook—when you strike your giant tarpon with a short jab of your stripping hand, this type of hook has a slightly better chance of "rotating" to the corner of the fish's mouth as it turns away. Bite tippets or leaders must be eighty to one hundred-pound test to absorb the running, jumping, and sandpaper-rough mouth of the silver king.

In an epic battle with any giant, you must use the finest equipment to achieve victory. Use the best brands of twelve-weight fly lines that are either floating or floating with a clear sink tip with a sink rate from 1.25 to 2.00 inches per second. Invest in as fine a fly rod as possible—ideally, a nine-foot, one-piece, twelve-weight graphite model.

Your reel should also be the finest equipment you can buy. When you obtain the finer fly reels, the drag will be smooth and strong. After you hook your giant and it begins to run, that drag should not seize up or overheat. The reel's line capacity should be three hundred yards of thirty-pound backing. Although you should not need all of this backing, it is good to know that a really big tarpon can be allowed to make a long, tiring, run without the worry that your trophy will spool you. Start off with about three pounds of drag "off the fly reel," and you can adjust it accordingly during the battle.

You are not alone in this epic quest. You will need the best of captains to guide you, advise you, and help you as much as ethically possible during the hunt and the fight. Your captain is not only your teacher and mentor but also your combat buddy and sometimes even a bit like a wise caddy. Your guide has a good deal of this already taken care of: step aboard the captain's six-hundred-pound poling skiff. It floats and runs in the shallowest shoals. The skiff is stocked with fully rigged fly outfits of the highest quality, sporting eight- or ten-kilogram class tippets. In its storage units are more than enough flies of all conceivable colors tied to their leaders. In your hunt and battle with the Homosassa giant tarpon, it is good to know you are part of a team.

Catching a giant tarpon takes two people. The angler usually mans the bow, standing on the deck or on an elevated casting platform. Some of these platforms have a backrest to help support and balance the angler. Some are simply flat, stand-alone platforms. In any event, it takes great physical endurance to stand for hours on end and be ready to cast at a moment's notice. It is also advantageous if the angler has excellent casting skills. It is a strategic asset for the team if the angler can cast far and accurately, because this allows presentation to the fish from farther away without spooking the quarry.

Giant Tarpon Lore

The largest fly-rod-caught tarpon weighed 202 pounds and came from the Homosassa area. Dozens of line class giant tarpon between 162 and 202 have been recorded in the International Game Fish Association record books, and this is why fly fishermen know about Homosassa. But it is an expensive price to pay for a tarpon record, because that tarpon must die in order to qualify its weight.

Perhaps the trend to kill tarpon in the larger sizes to chance a record will eventually lose its appeal—the tarpon of 202 pounds took twenty years to beat out a 188-pound fish. Some record chasers want to land an eighty-pound tarpon on six-pound test, yet the inevitably long battle might run the risk of undersize fish turning into shark bait.

The Gentlemen's Rules of Homosassa Tarpon Fishing

The rules of the game in this fishery may seem a bit strict, and they are, because giant tarpon fishing on the fly is a bit like Wimbledon. The top anglers who come here make thoughtful and difficult rules to challenge themselves and give the fish some winning odds.

The rule of sportsmanship for tarpon fishing is to fight the fish very hard, bring it to the boat within thirty minutes, and release it without touching the fish. If you are not sweating and breathing hard during the battle, chances are you are just "walking the dog." Since anglers and guides are both human and would-be heroes, almost everyone has broken this rule and fought the fish to exhaustion because it was huge and had world-record potential.

Novice anglers have no idea how much pressure they need to put on a tarpon to break its will. Have a friend hold a fish scale tied off to your fly tackle, and try to put seven to eight pounds of pressure on the scale and hold it—you will find this is very difficult. Keep your fighting pressure "to the max," and your tarpon will actually pull the weight of the skiff along: this will tire the fish out.

Gentlemen's Rules dictate that the goal of the battle is to get the first knot into the tip-top eye of the rod, to consider your quarry a "caught" fish. That is when the tarpon needs to be released. First, tighten the fly line and hold the reel spool stationary so that it will not revolve. Then yank the line forcefully in the opposite direction to break the leader off and end the battle. The rules also guide us to be strict, yet cautious, in the following instances. We avoid putting a giant tarpon in the boat because we want it to live. We avoid lip-gaffing a tarpon because the hole in its mouth hampers its feeding ability. We avoid holding a tarpon vertical out of the water to pose for pictures so as not to damage the jaws, roe, or internal organs of the fish.

While fighting tarpon, we employ two more strategies that may help keep our fish well hooked but in a shortened, more effective battle. When your tarpon goes airborne, always bow to the silver king by extending your rod arm horizontally toward the jumping fish. This gives the necessary slack to avoid pulled hooks or broken line with the sudden "weight gain," jumping, and head shaking of the fish. If your tarpon is a smaller fish of less than ninety pounds, or if it is a somersaulting, off-balance fish, come tight with extra pressure as soon as it lands so that it builds up more lactic acid and tires more quickly.

For starters, you have already hired a good guide who knows the business and knows where the fish are. To have the best chance, you must be ready to go early. Early in the morning, the tarpon are either milling about or are already daisy chaining as the sun rises over the tree line; however, occasional brisk winds can hamper surface spotting the tarpon. This is when you "wait it out" and leave around 9:00 a.m. By 10:00 a.m. the sun is getting up in the sky and will light up your fishing territory, which is only about six feet deep and crystal clear.

You will generally have three choices of fishing hours: leaving and returning early (5:00 a.m. to 1:00 p.m.), a standard day (8:00 a.m. to 4:00 p.m.), or a long day of ten to eleven hours. Although many guides do not offer eleven-hour trips, if they have an angler who is skilled and the fishing is hot, the guides will push their energy limits for the longer day, providing the angler pays for the extra time. Among experienced guides, charter costs range from $450 to $600 a day, with extra hours ranging from $50 to $100.

Tarpon Fleet Fishing Ethics

In the pursuit, poling, and casting for tarpon, ethical concerns are generally self-policed among the fleet of guides and the few recreational anglers. The rules are not written down, and you learn as you go. The rules can also change based on conditions and what the collective appraisals of the guides are on any given day.

Weekends are interesting and should be avoided if you are seriously tarpon fishing on the fly. They are, however, a great time to learn what tarpon fishing is all about. You can get a few good shots in before midmorning if you go early and beat the crowd. Because of this area's location, the through-traffic is never really bad.

Members of the fleet know one another by boat color and shape. A newcomer entering the fishing grounds with a poling platform and a pushpole is bound by the rules. Guides here go one step further than their counterparts in South Florida and the Florida Keys. Stern twin-trolling motors provide propulsion in lieu of poling. We consider this a good sign that these anglers are serious about their sport.

Within the fleet there is plenty of murmuring about using the trolling motors too much or moving about with too much speed. The fishery is sensitive enough that one or two boats running their large outboards around the fishing grounds can ruin an entire day of flats fishing. Although everyone must come and go by a large outboard, the rule of thumb the fleet expects from fellow anglers is to never run the outboard within a half mile of a poling boat. Idling the outboard slowly is tolerated but frowned upon, and idling away from the fleet toward the west is the safest route to exit.

Every day the conditions change and the routes of the tarpon differ; however, there is a general area where the boats start. If a guide is first to an area, that boat's position is generally respected by the others, who begin upwind about a half mile away, minimum. Guides may work in two fleets and fish two separate wads of tarpon. A good guide will either pole slowly or stake out to wait for passing tarpon. Certain areas in the fishery are fabulous for staking out or anchoring.

For years, the area has been divided into a fishery to baitcast exclusively and a fishery to fly fish exclusively. These are again Gentlemen's Rules, and sometimes exceptions are made, with either side changing tactics to produce a tarpon for a client. No one owns a deed to this property—it belongs to all of us. We all would like to have it to ourselves, but we must learn to get along and be good sportsmen.

Homosassa is still a small town. Old Homosassa, down on the river, is a quaint fishing village that is serene and quiet during the week. A few places offer lodging right on the river, including MacRae's of Homosassa and the Riverside Inn. For anglers who want to play golf and fly fish, the Plantation Inn of Crystal River has excellent amenities.

At the end of each season, fly fishing anglers from throughout the country and abroad count down the number of days until the next annual tarpon pilgrimage. This is a small fraternity of people who share a passion, anticipation, and excitement that never dulls. Each year produces another successful fly that hangs on a framed portrait of a bright sunrise with a huge tarpon jumping and the angler in the foreground. Each picture carries a story that is sure to sparkle the eye of anyone who will listen.

Flats Hot Spot: A Sight Fisherman's Paradise

A special area in my home waters is a submerged beach with a few scattered rocks that serve as markers for the guides and as routes for the tarpon. It is about three square miles. This hot spot is a sight fisherman's paradise because the black tarpon backs appear over sand that is off-white with a yellowish green tint. If the tarpon are not on the bottom—which is rare—they are cruising at approximately three miles per hour, either in a single-file "string" or in a group three to five fish wide and one hundred fish long. Some schools consist of two hundred or more tarpon, which we call "rolling Henrys." Tides have a fluctuation of about three feet under normal conditions. Low tides offer a good opportunity to find the tarpon in holes or farther off-shore.

Flats Tip: Explore Homosassa with a Guide

The Homosassa flats are not merely the Mecca for trophy-sized Florida tarpon. These shallows are an intricate habitat of rivers, channels, shallows, and rocky areas not easily navigated by neophytes with flats boats. It is essential to fish and learn with an expert local tarpon guide for success and familiarity on the Homosassa tarpon flats.

8

Permit

With Captain Tom Rowland

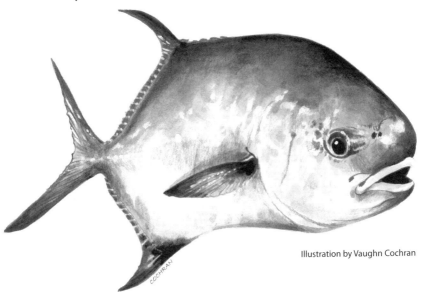

Illustration by Vaughn Cochran

Permit (*Trachinotus falcatus*)

Size Range: 5 to 56 pounds

Florida State Record: 56 pounds, 2 ounces

Florida Habitat: Offshore wrecks, beaches, channels, sand and rocky flats from Miami to the Marquesas

Baits: Live crabs, live shrimp, flathead hackle jigs, crab-style flies

Tackle: 10-pound spinning and baitcasting; 9- to 10-weight fly

Permit Hot Spots: Some of the largest permit in the world cruise the crystal flats west of Key West. Quicksilver grows to over fifty pounds in this tropical paradise!

Possibly you have been waiting all your life to hunt for and catch the fabled permit. Maybe you have read about them, seen a show on television, or witnessed a brief encounter as an iridescent shadow rocketing across some marine shallows. Whatever your prior experience, there is only one precious area in the American Gulf and Atlantic flats in which to pursue this grail: Florida's stretch of crystal clear shallows from Miami to the Marquesas. I call this area the Permit Coast.

The bonefish is often called the gray ghost; perhaps we could call the permit the silver shadow. True to that name, permit are spectral and always on the move.

They might be cruising a sandy flats edge in search of a blue crab ambling along the bottom. As soon as a permit spots this armored morsel, it rushes down, pins its prey to the bottom, and sucks the sweet meat out of the crushed shell. If the water is shallow enough, perhaps the permit's black sickle of a tail may have popped through the surface, giving a scepter's clue of its kingly presence.

Moments later, the permit might swim into an emerald-colored channel and continue its hunt. If the tide or wind is brisk, perhaps some yellow-green weed lines have formed, and the permit will pulse and flash along the surface, bumping the seaweed clumps to harvest multicolored shrimps. If some rocky or reefy rubble juts up from the flats floor, this predator is sure to have a look in search of a small lobster it can coax out of the crevices for dessert.

On-the-go permit are luminescent in their vigilance: their bright-sided flanks may be visible to the big sharks of the flats; therefore, permit always keep close to the safety of adjacent deeper channels or ocean. Bonefish feed on the flats in a grazing pick-up-go-down style, but permit are the elusive hunters—here, there, then who knows where? They are quicksilver.

Florida's Permit Coast is the planetary destination of choice for anglers seeking trophy specimens and world records of this marvelous species. My own angling career bears this out. I caught a twenty-three-pound, fifteen-ounce permit on four-pound line off Miami's Elliot Key that turned out to be a world record with the International Game Fish Association. A few years later in exotic Key West, I was fishing with Captain Bill Curtis on the "antenna" flats right across the harbor. We both saw a huge shadow wagging its way toward us sixty feet off our bow. Just as Bill called out the fish's position, my live crab bait was airborne, landing a good six feet in front of this awesome fish. The take was instantaneous.

I gave the fish a bit of line and struck hard. My rod bowed down hard as the ten-pound test line melted off my reel at an alarming rate. Bill racked his pushpole and cranked up the engine in pursuit of the fish. Just as my reel was about to be stripped of all its line, the boat was moving forward and I cranked in some of my now precious nylon connection. The fish took us three hundred yards to another flat on our "Key West-Nantucket" sleigh ride. We were able to regain line and stayed about forty feet above and on top of the fish to keep up the pressure and avoid any seesaw cutoffs by drop-offs or sea fans. The fish reversed its path and came to the surface. We could both see that it was a trophy.

Suddenly it went down and ran like a freight train back toward Key West Harbor. This back-and-forth fight lasted another thirty minutes, and the fish grew weaker as it circled the now idling boat. I was able to bring the fish alongside Bill's skiff, and he grabbed the permit firmly by the tail and into the boat. We both saw the size of the fish and Bill immediately ran his skiff back to the land-based weigh station in Garrison Bight. Within a half hour, my fish pulled down the Key West Fishing Tournament scale to thirty-seven and a half pounds and was the eventual winner in the spinning division.

Four magical years later in a mythical Key West, I landed a forty-two-pound monster on a live crab and jig combination right in Key West Harbor with Captain Bruce Cronin. Though this last catch was about a few hundred yards off the flats in deeper water, it clearly shows that Key West and the area to the west is just about dead-center on the map for giant permit.

Savvy anglers know they will best realize their dreams if they utilize the most knowledgeable local experts. I was able to enlist world-renowned Captain Tom Rowland of Key West to share his expertise, advice, techniques, and experience in helping anglers attain dreams of catching a permit on Florida's flats.

The Nature and Habits of a Permit, by Captain Tom Rowland

The permit is a misunderstood fish in my opinion. Fly fishermen have skillfully painted a picture of a permit as the wariest and often most impossible fish that swims anywhere. Many of these characteristics are *sometimes* true but not always. Permit are wary because they are offshore fish that have learned about the shallow water of the flats offering a buffet of morsels they can hardly resist.

As a species, permit generally school in water of twenty feet or deeper; they are quite at home in water 150 feet deep or more. When these fish venture onto the flats, they are understandably on edge as they feast on the offerings and try not to get too wrapped up in the choices and quantity to notice the big lemon shark in the distance. Often the permit on the flats are solitary fish without the comfort of a large school surrounding them.

In a foreign place, the permit is the least comfortable of all the inhabitants. Sharks, rays, barracuda, and bonefish have all adapted to this environment and sport hydrodynamic body styles that allow for high-speed maneuverability in inches of water. The permit is a tall, round fish visiting an area reserved for fish that can happily feed, escape, and live in water much shallower than they can. Its body style keeps the permit from ever being completely at home on the flats. Permit may feed on the flats all day or through an entire tide, but they are always ready for the quickest escape at the slightest hint of danger.

In Key West, anglers can fish for permit in all seasons, all conditions, and with all types of tackle. This area lends itself to fishing for this species much of the year. Permit are found in many places throughout the world, but no locales can compare to the lower Florida Keys in the habitat and numbers of large fish.

Permit need several things to thrive. A productive inshore or flats fishery for permit must have an excellent offshore fishery with coral heads, wrecks, reefs, and other offshore structures in nearby deep waters. In addition, the area must have extensive turtle grass flats and beds that are partially exposed during the lowest tides and submerged two to four feet by the highest tides. These extensive acreages provide a smorgasbord of food items and draw the fish onto the flats. Hard coral areas must be interspersed throughout the grass beds, and the water must be of the temperature that permit favor—a low of sixty degrees and a high around ninety-two degrees. The temperatures that permit like the best are between seventy-three and eighty-five degrees. To top it all off, the water must be clear for most or all of the year, not for the permit's sake but for the angler to be able to fish for them.

In the Key West area, all necessary criteria are present and offer fantastic permit fishing through vast areas. In places that lack even one or two of these characteristics, fishing for permit is marginal.

Permit are a difficult fish to catch, but often not as difficult as bonefish or tarpon. With the right approach, permit can be caught with more frequency than either of the other two members of the fabled "Grand Slam."

Permit Tackle

To be successful in catching permit under all conditions, anglers need to have mastered many skills with various types of tackle. I find that a fly rod and a spinning rod will cover most conditions, but anglers who enjoy baitcasting can also have success.

Rods

If you want to maximize your chances at permit, the spinning rod is unquestionably the most useful tool available. The spinning rod allows you to cast small and large crabs, light artificial lures and jigs, and live shrimp in every kind of circumstances. In the Florida Keys, we experience seasonal changes that require me to alter my spinning tackle to optimize the conditions. For example, winter and spring are often windy—a condition that allows guides to get very close to the fish before they become alarmed. The rough conditions camouflage anglers and boats.

In rough conditions I use a seven-foot medium-action spinning rod designed for eight- to seventeen-pound line or twelve- to twenty-pound line to throw crabs that measure two to three inches across the carapace. The rod needs to have enough backbone to fight and land a fish of over thirty pounds, yet have a tip sensitive and light enough to be able to present these baits accurately and precisely in windy condi tions. Casting distance is not the most important aspect of the setup at this time of year, so I choose a rod that I am comfortable casting and that can whip a large fish easily.

As the season wears on, I find that the conditions become calmer—at least we experience more calm days. As a general rule of thumb, the calmer the conditions, the spookier the fish will be; therefore, the longer the cast required to achieve success. Simply changing a few things in your tackle can easily add ten to fifty feet to your cast. A rod that measures seven and a half feet and that employs a lighter and more responsive tip will out-cast a seven-foot rod with the same line and lure. As the season becomes calmer and the fish become more wary, I go to a seven-and-a-half-foot, medium-action rod designed for six- to twelve-pound line. The extra length and whippy tip will throw lighter crabs successfully, which is often necessary to present the bait to the fish without alarming it. During these calmer conditions, choose a crab measuring two to two-and-a-half inches across the carapace.

The Florida Keys weather in the summer is dead calm. Often the ocean is as calm as a millpond, making it tough to sneak up on permit; however, summer is also the time when permit are most plentiful. To take advantage of the calm conditions, I change my tackle and use an eight-foot medium-light action rod with four- to eight-pound line. These rods will cast an even smaller crab a country mile. I routinely use the smallest crabs I can throw, which might measure from one to two inches across the carapace. On the smallest crabs, a split shot is often necessary. Fighting a fish on a noodle rod like the one mentioned is much like fighting a fish on a fly rod.

Reels

The reel choice for permit does not necessarily change from season to season. Anglers need a compact reel capable of holding 230 to 300 yards of ten-pound test monofilament based on the manufacturer's specifications. Reels of this size are often categorized as size forty or 4,000 among the tackle manufacturers. The capacity is important but not as important as the drag or ability to withstand the harsh marine conditions. A front drag is standard; rear drag models repeatedly fail. The drag should be ceramic and lubricated and checked often before attempting to catch a permit.

Because saltwater destroys most spinning reels, it is important to choose one from a company dedicated to saltwater fishing. The reel should have six to ten ball bearings and a finish that does not corrode in salt water. The bail system needs to be well thought-out and designed for the saltwater environment. Coiled springs have proven to be less effective than the newly established magnets as triggers for optimal bail functioning. This durable magnet system is impervious to salt water and has shown great success.

Line

The line choice definitely varies from season to season. In the past, ten-pound monofilament was standard for most of the year. Twelve-pound was used in the winter, when casting distance is generally shorter, and eight-pound was used in the summer when longer casts are necessary. In some situations, monofilament is still the best choice, but the revolution of braided lines has made those situations fewer and farther between.

The advantage of braided lines over monofilament is that the diameter of a braided line of equal-pound test is greatly reduced. A braided line of thirty-pound test will be the same diameter as eight-pound test monofilament, whereas eight-pound braid has the diameter of two-pound monofilament. Many situations in permit fishing require that anglers cast as far as they can in order to reach these wary fish. Braided lines immediately add distance to the cast without making a single change in technique. For permit, I prefer the handling and casting ability of the fourteen-, twenty-, and thirty-pound braided lines. These lines have enough diameter to behave like ten-pound monofilament yet are stronger and cast farther than ordinary monofilament.

In the winter I use thirty-pound braid on most of my reels because it casts a long way, and due to the abrasion resistance and strength, I do not have to change the line often. Sometimes I use thirty-pound braid as my casting line and use it with a (clear) ten-pound fluorocarbon leader to make the fight more sporting. As conditions calm down and casts have to be longer, I switch to fourteen- or twenty-pound braided line. In the summer, I switch back to eight- or ten-pound braided line.

Other advantages that greatly improve permit fishing include the ability of braided line to be twisted and still perform well. Often beginning anglers and even experienced anglers using monofilament will reel against the drag during the fight, resulting in line that is totally unusable after only one fish. Carrying spare spools preloaded with fresh line became standard but required a lot of preparation time. After a productive day of fishing, the line had to be stripped off and replaced with fresh line due to nicks, abrasions, and twists. With braid, the line will still become twisted, but the braided line behaves well and remains fishable no matter how badly it has been twisted.

Leaders

Besides their many advantages, braided lines do have some disadvantages. First and foremost, the line is visible in the water. Tying braid directly to the hook or lure is not a good idea because the fish can easily see it, and any fish that is at all leader-shy will reject the offering. To overcome this problem, we simply use a leader of fluorocarbon line attached to the braided line with a double Uni-Knot. The leader should be between two and four feet long. The pound test is up to the angler and can vary from two- to thirty-pound leader. I like ten- or twelve-pound fluorocarbon for a leader because it is virtually invisible in the water and allows the bait to swim freely.

Baits

Bait choices are easy. Permit will eat anything as long as it is a live crab. Joking aside, that could be considered the truth in most situations. As already indicated, I like to throw the smallest crab I can, given the conditions. I have seen permit reject crabs that are too large. Less frequently, I have seen permit reject crabs that are too small. The most important aspect of a live crab is that it is alive, so hook them carefully and as far to the edge of the carapace as possible. Once hooked, keep the crab in the water at all times so that it will be fresh and active when you toss it in front of the permit of a lifetime. Permit will eat a dead crab on occasion but often reject them. Live and fresh crabs presented correctly are rarely refused.

Shrimp

Live shrimp are also a good bait choice and are responsible for many permit catches each year. The shrimp has to be large enough to throw the distance required. I often choose a shrimp over a crab in areas where I see both permit and bonefish. Split shot will help throw the baits farther if placed directly above the hook.

Jigs

Jigs are productive and are used if bait is not available or if anglers want more of a challenge. Standard quarter-ounce flat-head jigs or wiggle jigs work well. For me, the most productive colors are yellow and white. In calm conditions, choose an eighth-ounce jig. Tipping the jig with a shrimp tail will improve your chances at permit.

Crab imitations

Tackle companies have begun to manufacture soft plastic crabs that are very realistic and can be productive for permit. The problem with these baits is that many of them lack adequate movement to simply cast the lure in front of a fish and wait. The angler has to impart action to the lure to get the bite. These baits are productively rigged on a one-eighth- to one-fourth-ounce jig head or rigged weedless on a standard worm hook with a bullet weight pegged to the line directly above the hook.

Techniques with a Spinning Rod

You must master several techniques to be successful with permit. First, maximize your casting distance. Casting with one hand on the rod will not suffice. Keep your top hand at the reel and the bottom hand at the terminal end of the handle. When you cast, your top hand will push the rod to the target while your bottom hand pulls the handle toward your body. The result is far greater loading ability in the rod and far greater casting distance.

Accuracy is also important and can be accomplished with the same technique. Place the index finger of your top hand on the rod pointing toward the target as you release the line from the "trigger finger."

Minimizing impact of the bait on the water can be accomplished by casting low and hard directly to the target. While the bait is on the way to the target, raise the rod to a twelve o'clock position and feather the line to minimize impact. With practice, you can easily make a live shrimp or live crab land as gently as a fly.

Fly Fishing

Fly fishing for permit is difficult, not because the fish are terribly difficult to catch but because our flies and techniques do not accurately represent what permit want to eat. Permit look at a dead crab the same as they look at a fly. The profile is interesting but not really what they had in mind. Flies need to have action resembling that of real crabs; until they do, permit will remain exceptionally difficult to catch on fly.

To get a permit to eat a fly, you need to master several casts and be prepared to deliver these casts to the target in a variety of situations. The best permit fly fishermen become comfortable with a twenty- to twenty-five-mile-per-hour wind at any angle and are able to get the fly to the target.

The flies currently being tied only resemble a live crab when the lead eyes are dragging the fly to the bottom. For this reason, you need to cast the fly directly in front of the permit so that the fish sees the fly escaping and it triggers the eating response.

Fly Rods and Reels

A nine-foot, ten-weight rod matched to a floating weight-forward line is the standard outfit. Leader length varies with conditions, but a nine- to twelve-foot leader tapered to twelve-pound test is standard.

The reel needs to be capable of holding two hundred yards of backing plus the WF10F line. Permit fight hard but will not stress the fly tackle like a tarpon, tuna, or sailfish. A quality reel designed for saltwater use should be fine as long as it has a disc drag made of cork or modern materials.

Specialty lines have been created for permit fishing, and they work well. These include severe weight-forward lines to aid the fly in turnover under windy conditions. Try them all, and use the line you cast the best.

Best Time of Year to Catch the Florida Keys Permit

The Florida Keys is truly a year-round permit fishery. Of course, some times are better than others for permit, but you can feel confident that with enough searching, you can find permit. My favorite times of the year are February, March, and June to November. The months of February and March coincide with the water temperatures climbing back into the permit's comfort zone and are just before the spawning season for permit. There are a lot of permit on the flats during this time, and the conditions are conducive to catching them on the fly. I look for days following a cold front when the sky is completely clear and the temperature is increasing. The windy conditions that usually accompany this meteorological scenario allow anglers to get close to the permit and require shorter casts.

I find the largest number of permit during the summer and fall, in and around structures and on the flats. The calm conditions of summer and fall require longer casts with both spin and fly; however, opportunity abounds.

During both times of year, I prefer a high tide of five feet or greater in the middle of the day. This allows me to fish virtually wherever I want and lets the permit frequent areas formerly inaccessible. We have a four- to six-hour tidal difference between the ocean and many areas of the backcountry, so many anglers make a big mistake by choosing the time to fish simply based on the tide chart. Each area has its own best tide, and discovering when that best tide occurs comes through many days spent researching these areas.

As a guide specializing in permit fishing, I am expected to find permit every day, so I have had to learn to fish effectively on all tides and conditions. I routinely tell anglers that tide is not as important as the time of year or skill level of the angler. In other words, a good angler is better off on the worst tides in August than after a debilitating cold front on the prime tides in December.

Taking a permit on fly can mean standing all day on a forward casting deck. That bow leaning post can really help steady your back in this quest. Photo by Scott Heywood/Angling Destinations.

Poling Strategies for Permit

The most important thing about permit fishing from a boat is to be quiet. Slamming hatches, noisy feet, and hull slap will prevent you from catching permit. Many anglers get sucked into the shallow water because they are not confident of finding the fish if their tails do not come out of the water. Tailing fish are fun and exciting, but they are more difficult to catch. I routinely fish in three to six feet of water and catch permit on every type of tackle. Approach slowly and quietly in areas in which you believe permit will be. Be ready to stop the boat quietly when you see the fish and position the boat for the best possible shot.

Flats boats are not the only type of boat in which you can have success. The new breed of bay boats also allow quality shots at permit. I use my Skeeter 24 Bay with a trolling motor to catch large numbers of permit throughout the year. It is important to have a mechanism to stop the boat. I have a Power Pole mounted on all of my boats, which allows silent stopping of the boat in extremely high winds. I suggest using the trolling motor as little as possible and on a consistent setting. Constant altering of the speed is alarming to the fish, but anglers can get very close to fish by keeping the motor on a low setting and taking their time moving in. Approach downwind and be ready to stop the boat when you see the fish. Stopping the boat creates distance between you and the fish and prevents the boat from inadvertently running over the quarry.

Advice about Booking a Fishing Guide

If you have never fished the Lower Keys it will serve you well to invest in a quality guide. Try to find someone who specializes in permit and has a good track record of catching them. If you would like to catch permit, I invite you to call me, as I love to fish for permit more than any other species.

Bait and Lure Placement

Under most conditions anglers need to cast the bait, fly, or lure very close to the fish and then let it drop. If the weather is completely calm, casting beyond the fish and bringing the offering to the fish quietly

This is the method for holding a permit. Photo by Scott Heywood/Angling Destinations.

and slowly may be the only way to get your quarry to see your presentation before it spooks.

Fighting a Permit

When a permit is first hooked, be ready for a long, hard run. Simply keep tension on the fish and keep the rod bowed deeply. Be ready for the fish to turn around quickly and suddenly and run back at you. Collect the line as quickly as possible and continue to keep tension on the fish throughout the fight. I do not recommend pulling exceptionally hard or keeping a heavy drag setting because permit will fight only as hard as they are being fought. In other words, when you pull very hard, the permit pulls back very hard. Pulling gently but firmly throughout the fight will cause the fish to run longer and more often, which will shorten the fight and help you land more fish.

Permit are found in abundance from the Seven Mile Bridge to the Marquesas. It is my opinion that the highest concentrations are found west of Key West, but my permit pursuits have taken me all over the Lower Keys during the course of the year in search of the very highest

A trophy flats-caught permit taken on a fly is the dream of a lifetime. Photo by Scott Heywood/Angling Destinations.

quality fishing. The lower Florida Keys offer the biggest permit on the planet. All of the required criteria for permit fishing combined with vast expanses of flats and low angling pressure result in the finest permit fishing in the world.

Flats Hot Spot: Permit Havens in the Keys

Permit can be found by starting at the southern tip of Key Biscayne at the Cape Florida Lighthouse and running the deeper water east of the flats all the way south past Soldier's Key until you get to Ragged Key 5. Consult the pertinent maps and be sure to fish in weather that is pleasant and warm enough to heat the water temperature to

Younger permit have more elongated dorsal and anal fins than do adults. Photo by Scott Heywood/Angling Destinations.

Rubble and rocky shorelines often support crab populations that lure in permit.
Photo by Scott Heywood/Angling Destinations.

seventy-five degrees or above. In addition, coordinate this to coincide with an incoming tide. When you arrive a few hundred yards east of Ragged Key 5 and nearby Boca Chita Key, scout for rock piles about one hundred yards offshore of the rocky flats inshore. They appear as slightly lighter patches underwater. When you find a rock pile, position yourself about sixty feet offshore and uptide of the structure. Let the area "settle down." You should eventually see permit during the last part of the incoming tide. Remember that the success of your hunt is predicated on weather that produces the type of conditions that cause permit to move in from offshore onto the rocky flats.

9

Sharks

With Captain Robert "RT" Trosset

Illustration by Vaughn Cochran

Sharks

Blacktip Shark (*Carcharhinus limbatus*)
Florida State Record: 152 pounds
Bull Shark (*Carcharhinus leucas*)
Florida State Record: 517 pounds
Lemon Shark (*Negoprion brevirostris*)
Florida State Record: 397 pounds
Florida Habitat: Offshore, inshore, and deeper oceanic flats from Miami to the Marquesas
Baits: Barracuda and bonito strips, plugs, and flies
Tackle: 12- to 15-pound spinning or baitcasting; 12–weight and higher fly
Shark Hot Spots: Monstrously large sharks—like bulls, lemons, blacktips, and hammerheads—swim the fertile and fabled shallows west of Key West.

Flats Fishing for Sharks, by Captain Robert "RT" Trosset

In my long career as a charter captain, some of my most exciting rec-ollections are my shark fishing adventures around the flats of Key West. I am proud to say that this part of Florida can lay claim to being the epicenter and origin of standardized light tackle and fly fishing for monster sharks in the shallows.

Sharks are the largest denizens of Florida's flats, some of them eas-ily dwarfing the largest tarpon. When you hook a monster shark in a few feet of water, you are truly in for a wild ride. Looking back on this fishery, the ride has been like a merry-go-round of exciting moments and memories. Images spin by, one after the other—a huge bull shark that almost succeeded in pulling me in with it when I sunk the gaff, the sweet moment of victory in catching a massive hammerhead on fly tackle, the breeze and briny scents while drifting along the flats of the Marquesas, and the day-starting joys of "bait fishing" for the bar-racuda that would later serve as overboard scent chum.

When I talk about large sharks in shallow water, consider this: in less than ten feet of water, I have landed bull sharks to 468 pounds; lemon sharks to 314 pounds; hammerheads to 398 pounds; and tiger sharks to 489 pounds. But I have also seen, hooked, and lost, for one reason or another, hammers and tigers challenging the 1,000-pound mark. In fact, the biggest tiger I have seen in shallow water we did not have a chance to lose. In the six feet of depth, the fish's back was out of the water and it was kicking up mud to get to us. No one wanted to catch it!

Rest assured that excitement and epic battles are the key words in shark fishing on the flats—we call them "the men in gray suits." Most anglers who experience this type of fishing leave feeling more like survivors than victors.

A South Florida Start

The beginning of shark fishing on the flats was born of the creativ-ity of light tackle anglers like Norman Duncan and Captain Ralph Delph. Sharks are among the largest fish ever taken on regulation fly tackle—even larger than the billfish that have been taken to date. Over the years, I have had the opportunity to develop and fine-tune light tackle techniques for a number of species, but it was Pat Ford who taught me how to shark fish.

Pat knew how to do it but did not have the boat or gaff man. He showed me everything he learned from fishing with other people. Our testing grounds were the shallow water flats surrounding Key West. I was very fortunate to have the opportunity to make a living and at the same time get an education from anglers like Ford and fellow angler Dr. Scott Russell. Over the years I have improved on what we knew twenty-five years ago, and I am glad to share it with you.

Bait Choices

The popular misconception about shark fishing is that you have to flood the water with blood and guts, á la Captain Quint from the Peter Benchley classic, *Jaws*. While that may be true in deep water, in

Sharks can threaten hooked bonefish. If this happens, back off on your drag and let the bonefish try to outrun the shark. Even then, the shark might win. Photo by Scott Heywood/Angling Destinations.

the shallows we prefer that a consistent scent path be generated by a single, favored food fish. This method can drive even the largest ones wild. With chumming for sharks on Florida's flats, often less is more.

In the Lower Keys, barracuda are the bait of choice, yet the options are excellent. If we are unable to procure 'cudas for bait—which is unusual—we use little tunny, jack crevalle, ladyfish, king mackerel, and a host of other species. In a pinch, even finely ground block chum will work.

One of the beauties of shark fishing Key West-style is that catching the bait can be as exciting as catching the target species. Look for 'cudas to inhabit shallow flats around schools of baitfish like glass minnows and pilchards. Key indicators include diving birds and jumping houndfish. The most effective method for catching barracuda is casting or trolling dead ballyhoo along the edges of the flats. Casting tube lures and other artificials is also effective, but remember that the key to hooking up is throwing them as far as you can and retrieving them as fast as humanly possible. I often tell my clients to wind as if you are trying to break the reel. This type of retrieve stimulates the pursuit reaction in a barracuda. Remember, warp speed—you simply cannot move the lure or ballyhoo fast enough to keep them away from it.

If you know you are going to be shark fishing in the future, it is possible to stock up on baits in your freezer. However, I have noticed over the years that a frozen bait does not seem to draw fish like a fresh one.

Shark Weather

Probably the three most important factors in successful sharking on the flats are wind, tide, and water temperature. I prefer the wind against the tide. That condition gives you the best coverage of the fishing: the boat is moving against the tide. As the scent trail is being carried out on the water flow, it goes away from the boat rather than "following" you; therefore, you are less likely to run over the scent, and this combination prevents premature encounters with approaching sharks.

The lower stages of the outgoing tide seem to be better. When fishing on the higher stages of the tide, you could be fishing on the crown or the middle of the flat while all the life forms are spread out. On the lower stages of the tide, all the shark's favorite food items are swept toward the edge, concentrating their hunting efforts.

When the water temperature is below seventy-two degrees the fish are hesitant. From seventy-six to seventy-eight degrees, they are fairly active. If the mercury rises above eighty-eight degrees, you will lose most species except for lemon sharks. The best fishing months in the Florida Keys run from the end of March until August.

Sharks are highly responsive to weather systems and are dependent on other life forms on Florida's flats. The major weather forces that tend to drive life off the flats are cold front blasts of chilly air that last long enough to drop the water temperatures; thus deep winter is not your best shark weather. Conversely, some flats produce good shark fishing during the hottest days of summer, provided the water levels are high enough. A passing Florida summertime thunderstorm does not seem to bother them if they have something to feed on. The warmth of spring brings throngs of life back to the flats of Florida. The sharks will be there waiting—so should you.

Setting up the Drift and Getting Ready for Battle

After catching your bait and arriving in the area you are going to fish, it is a fairly simple matter to set up your drift. Boat position is critical. Most of our fishing is done from center console or flats boats. Position the boat to sit somewhat square into the wind but with the bow trailing off in the direction that the scent corridor is going. This prevents hull obstruction and turbulence from disrupting the scent trail.

One way to accomplish this drift is to trim the outboard motors up and turn them into the wind. The engine acts as a sail and the reduced drag of the lifted lower unit will push the stern off the wind and the bow onto it.

Getting started with your overboard chum fish can be as simple as putting a rope through the gills and mouth of the bait; however, I prefer to make a shark rope out of a six-foot length with a metal carabiner clip attached to the business end. That clip will penetrate the lower jaw of the baitfish, yet is impervious to teeth—those of the bait and the shark.

Chum Bait Management

It is necessary to cut the bait in order to get the scent trail started. Something I have learned over the years is that when you butterfly the baitfish (basically filleting to a fourth of the way or halfway down the side of the fish and leaving it hanging), cut the trailing edge of the butterflied piece into four or five fingers. This increases the surface area available to produce scent, while preserving more of the bait for use later in the day.

Before cutting more of the baitfish, scrape the backbone, puncture the internal organs, and whack the flesh and skin with the fillet knife to release a much more dynamic scent of blood, bits of flesh, scales, and bile from the organs into the water. It makes a tremendous difference.

Regardless of the type of tackle you are using—light, heavy, natural bait, artificial, or fly—it is best to try to hook the shark on its initial pass at the boat. Be aware that on the shark's first charge, he is coming in to eat. On subsequent passes, the fish may become increasingly wary.

If the sharks become wary, try removing the bait from the water entirely. As the scent trail fades, so will the fish. But put the bait back in after about ten minutes of drifting without it, and you will see a definite change in the sharks' attitudes as they return to the now replenished scent.

Above all, pay attention! While it is easy to be lulled into complacency or distraction on our beautiful Florida flats, when you wait for a fish to come in to the chum, you cannot let down your guard. It is hard to believe that a four-hundred-pound fish can sneak up on your boat in four feet of water, but it happens routinely. This runs the risk they will tear up your chum bait, which is why it is a good idea to have one or two spare baits in reserve.

Artificial, Fly Tackle, and Bait Considerations

When fishing fly or artificials, anglers must anticipate the shark's movements. Make your presentation in front and to the side of the fish so that you can be sure it will see the bait. A shark's eyesight is generally very poor, so it is important to put the lure or fly where the fish will see it and intercept it.

When battling sharks on fly and light tackle, the most important thing you can do is watch which side of the fish's mouth the hook comes to rest in. If you can fight the fish from that side, your chances of success—particularly with fly—increase dramatically.

I first learned that lesson when fishing with marine artist Mike Stidham years ago. After hooking and losing more than twenty-five hammerhead sharks on fly, I decided we needed to shove the rod tip underwater and bring the twelve-inch bite tippet under and behind the fish's hammer-shaped head. Stidham executed the move perfectly, and after forty minutes I gaffed and boated one of the most difficult fish to subdue with a straight gaff. It became the first hammerhead ever taken on fly tackle in accordance with the stringent rules of the International Game Fish Association.

The majority of flats fishing we do for sharks is with the fly rod, due to the growing popularity of saltwater fly fishing. The fish are cooperative and generally are not too picky about presentations—a perfect combination for anyone who wants to learn how to fly fish in salt water.

Any high-quality twelve-weight or larger rod will do. My personal favorites are the travel rods made by Abel. They are some of the toughest fly rods I have ever used, and they have incredible lifting power. I always try to use the heaviest fly outfit possible. In some situations you can get away with nine- or ten-weight rods, but invariably, when you limit yourself to a lighter rod, that is when the two-hundred-pounder shows up.

I am also a big fan of the Abel reels. I prefer direct-drive models like the Super 12 or 4.5N.

Floating fly lines work best, keeping the fly out of the bottom and up in the water column. I like to modify them by cutting them down to eighty feet in length from the back end. This allows you to pack more backing on the reel and also reduces the drag created by the fly line moving through the water. For backing, I prefer PowerPro braided line in fifty-pound test. It is equivalent to twenty-pound Dacron backing, greatly increasing the line-carrying capacity of the reel.

Look at those teeth! Always use a wire leader with sharks. Photo by Captain Ted Lund.

For bull, tiger, hammerhead, and lemon sharks, any color streamer fly will work, as long as it is orange. The fish seem to like this color and it is easy to see. Large deceiver-style patterns work best, particularly when tied on 4/0 Mustad 3407 SS or 7766 hooks.

For blacktip sharks, one of the most exciting species you can fish for, I prefer a chartreuse or chartreuse and orange streamer. My good friend and fly fishing expert Captain Ted Lund (now editor of *Fly Fishing in Salt Waters* magazine) began experimenting with blacktips and other species and found that the blacktip and spinner sharks preferred the bright green or combination streamers over solid orange. He even had better luck with plugs colored in similar schemes.

For fishing with artificials or lures, I prefer twelve-, fifteen- and twenty-pound outfits. My current favorites are made by Okuma tackle. Although I use lighter tackle most of the time, I always have a fifty- or eighty-pound standup outfit ready to go. It is important to have one rhino-killer outfit rigged and ready—just in case.

If I am fishing with bait, I float several chunks of 'cuda on balloons while drifting. This is an incredibly effective method for attracting and hooking flats sharks, and lets you know exactly where the bait is at all times.

Terminal Tackle

Over the years I have developed some different ideas about the terminal tackle required for sharks. Obviously, one important link in the chain is wire. For fly and other artificial applications, I prefer fifty-eight-pound test coated Steelon wire. Not only does the material lend itself to easier knot tying, but the multistrand wire fits into the gaps between the teeth of most sharks, preventing them from chewing through the bite tippet or leader.

For class tippet, I prefer a hard, abrasion-resistant monofilament, such as Rio's International Gamefish Association Fishing class tippet. You lose very few fish to chafing with such material. In classic tippet construction form, I double each end of the line with a Spider Hitch or Bimini Twist, leaving a single strand of tippet about two feet in length between the knots. I tie a Surgeon's loop in one of the doubles, which connects to the butt section. The other double line goes to the wire leader with an Albright or triple Surgeon's knot.

For bait fishing, I prefer a rod length of eighty-pound Berkley Vanish fluorocarbon leader material knotted to a two- or three-foot shot of Malin's 108-pound hard wire leader. In a pinch, you can double over lighter wire leader and twist it to provide more strength and bite resistance. I connect the terminal end to the heavy mono leader with an Albright knot, then use a haywire twist to connect the wire to an 8/0 double-strength 3407 SS.

Fighting Tactics

It is important with sharks—as with any game fish—to stay on the same side of the fish as the side where it is hooked. A 368-pound mako shark caught off Key West by JoJo Hemberger and Captain Greg Sherertz several years ago on a three-hundred-pound monofilament leader illustrates the importance of that strategy. Sherertz caught that fish while swordfishing after a lengthy discussion about how Mike Stidham and I collected the first hammerhead taken on fly.

In shallow water, hooked sharks usually head even shallower. Keep pressure on the fish at all times and be alert to its attitude; one thing sharks share in common is that they will attack the boat when they feel it is a threat to them.

Pulitzer Prize–winning author and world-class angler Phil Caputo tells a story about being thrown into the water by a famous Key West captain who jammed his throttle into reverse to avoid the wrath of an incoming three-hundred-pound bull shark.

"The next thing I knew, I was the only thing between a three-hundred-pound shark and the boat," says Caputo. "I did a standing leap back in the boat, and never even got wet."

Try to avoid putting yourself—or others—in that position.

Releasing, Boating, and Gaffing Sharks

If you just want to release your catch, it is a simple matter of breaking the fish off boatside, making sure to break the leader as close to the fish as possible. If you'd like to get a picture of your catch—as we often do with small blacktips and lemons—an Aftco tailer will help you subdue and boat the fish for a few quick snapshots. Just be sure to avoid the biting end.

For record or tournament anglers, things get a little more serious. For fly and light tackle catches, I prefer to use an eight-foot, custom-built fiberglass gaff with a machined, three-inch gap hook manufactured by Top Shot of Australia.

When straight gaffing, it is important to have a second or third gaff man to back you up, especially with the larger sharks. Much of the common practice over the years has been to hit the fish in the tail, although I have found hitting them in the gill area is most effective for two reasons. First, the only soft area on a shark is around the gills. Second, when you have its head out of the water, you have its complete attention.

For larger fish on heavier tackle, standard flying gaffs will work, although I prefer to keep the rope length short, just enough to let me reach the fish. Try to stick the fish in the gills or shoulder area and you should have it easy from there. In either scenario, I prefer to lash

Captain "RT" Trosset—the chap with the well-known beard—and his angler with a trophy lemon shark taken on fly tackle. Photo by Captain Ted Lund.

the fish to the outside of the boat for the ride home, limiting your exposure to the thrashing, the sandpaper-like skin, and the gnashing teeth.

After having them chew on the rub rails and leave teeth marks on the gunwales of several of my boats, and attack the lower units of my outboards, there are few fish I get as excited about as flats sharks. Give them a try and I'll bet you'll be as hooked as I am. You might just end up feeling like a heroic survivor—as in the television show of that name.

Flats Hot Spot: Battling Sharks in Stiltsville

While you await your Madison Square Garden encounter with the monster sharks of Key West under the guidance of captain-trainers like Robert "RT" Trosset, you can practice on your own. The flats south of Biscayne Bay's Stiltsville offer plenty of shark action during summer. As the last half of the incoming tide begins, stake out your skiff on a stern cleat uptide of one of the deeper flats, preferably with a channel nearby. Butterfly a barracuda or small bonito and affix it to a rope attached to your bow cleat. Let the scent do its work long enough, and your light tackle battle with the brawler in the sharkskin trunks should soon begin!

10

Barracuda

With Captain Jon Cooper

Illustration by Vaughn Cochran

Barracuda (*Sphyraena barracuda*)
Size Range: 5 to 50 pounds
Florida State Record: 67 pounds
Florida Habitat: Offshore, inshore, and flats from Miami to the Marquesas
Baits: Live mullet, pinfish, blue runners, plugs, tube lures, and flies
Tackle: 10- to 12-pound spinning and baitcasting; 10-weight fly
Barracuda Hot Spots: Trophy barracuda abound on the deeper Atlantic and
    Gulf flats surrounding the Lower Keys and Key West.

Fishing for Barracuda, by Captain Jon Cooper

The name barracuda conjures up visions of voraciousness. Thoughts of big eyes and even bigger teeth gloss the memory of anyone who has ever snorkeled the crystal clear waters of our beautiful Florida flats or coral reefs. The barracuda's real name is the great barracuda, and great it is. This is not just a name but a title, like "your honor," "your majesty," "your eminence," or just plain "sir."

Deservedly so, the great barracuda is the dominant figure on the shallow water scene, stepping aside only to the shark in terms of terrible threat to the unwary. It hovers in big-brother posture, policing the area. In what seems a nanosecond, it strikes like lightning. Its razor-like teeth slash and slice in a most efficient manner, leaving only a blood plume and perhaps a few fish parts to sink slowly into waiting arms of the flats-dwelling crabs. The barracuda is highly aggressive, highly efficient, and highly motivated.

These characteristics make for the best of sport. Nothing can compare to the visual effects of the barracuda's warp-speed attacks, violent strikes, and skyrocketing jumps. It is sport fish supreme. It will terrorize you and peg your fun meter all at once.

For many flats anglers, one of the greatest qualities of a game fish is participation, without which fishing would have nothing to do with catching or releasing. The great barracuda is most accommodating in this regard. Many a day of flats fishing is highlighted by the willingness of 'cudas—big and small—to take an offering even in the most adverse conditions. Of all the flats species, you will find this wonderful fish is by far the most reliable.

The feeding habit of the great barracuda is one of crafty ambush. It loves to hide alongside island shorelines, rock piles, and shallow water wrecks. These areas also attract lots of food fish, which often fall prey to his majesty when he lunges out of the shadows to snare and snip prey. Indeed, every shoalwater ambush point in his kingdom from Miami to Key West has the potential for flats fishing for the great barracuda.

Tackle Types for Barracuda

Another wonderful thing about the great barracuda is that you can use spinning, plug, or fly tackle with good results when fishing for his majesty on the flats. Your choice should be based on the tackle with which you feel most skilled and comfortable, so that you can get the most strikes and hookups. Each class of tackle has its own special characteristics, advantages, and disadvantages. With spinning and plug casting on the flats, usually you will be casting and retrieving tube lures, wooden "swish" plugs, or undulating soft plastic jerk baits. At times it may be necessary to retrieve your lure extremely fast to entice the barracuda to strike it. Retrieve speed of the various tackle

Barracuda this size fight magnificently on the flats. Photo by Scott Heywood/ Angling Destinations.

types is discussed later. Occasionally, the great barracuda will strike a moderately retrieved artificial, but generally when you cast lures with spin or plug tackle for 'cuda on the flats, your tackle must be capable of very rapid retrieves.

It is almost inevitable that you will encounter enormous barracuda on the flats that will refuse all artificial lures and flies. That may be the time to utilize tackle capable of handling live baits. Generally, this will involve casting a live bait—like a small pinfish—with spinning tackle. Another method I have developed and use with great effectiveness on the Florida flats is quietly trolling a live bait on twenty-pound plug tackle using my bow-mounted electric trolling motor. These two methods have resulted in far more trophy flats-caught 'cuda than standard casting with lures or flies.

Spinning tackle is the most popular tackle for casting to barracuda on the flats. It is the easiest tackle type to master and is capable of the most rapid casts. Spinning tackle casts farther and is more reliable in powering a cast directly into the wind than plug or fly tackle. Spinning tackle is most often capable of the fastest retrieves because it affords the highest ratio of line retrieved per crank of the handle. High-speed tackle capacity is essential for casting for barracuda on the flats. If you are flats fishing from Miami to the Marquesas, it always pays to keep a fast-retrieve spinner handy in case you have a 'cuda encounter. Choose spinning reels with retrieve ratios of five to one or higher. Longer rods are associated with longer casts, so choose a spinning rod at least seven or seven and a half feet in length, making sure the rod strength maintains itself as the rod gets longer. Spinning reels—because of the perpendicular line retrieval system—run the risk of line twist for monofilament lines if the angler reels while the fish is running line off the reel's drag. This will not be the slightest problem if you do not reel when your drag is going out. The newer microbraid lines will not stay twisted even if the angler reels against a running drag.

Plug tackle has three advantages when battling a barracuda on the flats, all of which combine to cut down your fighting time and release your fish much sooner. Because of the revolving spool and direct line retrieval system, you can reel continuously without the threat of twisted line common to spinning tackle. Saltwater baitcasting or "plug" reels, as they are known in Florida, are capable of handling and casting heavier lines than comparable spinning reels. Combine a "winching" retrieve with a heavier drag setting and heavier line, and you can appreciate the pressure you will be putting on the barracuda to yield in the battle and hasten his release. Although barracuda do not run for the cover of structures that are readily available to them, their runs can be quite long and take your line across and into sea fan country. The winch power of plug tackle will go a long way in minimizing those runs.

Whether used as casting tackle in the hands of an expert, or as a slow-troll or still-fish live bait reel for a novice, plug tackle excels in lure manipulation, hook-setting power, and ease of operation. The way you hold and position a plug rod in your hand creates a potential for your wrist to give your lure finesse and a twitching motion that is truly unique to this type of tackle. In addition, it should be clear that striking and fighting your barracuda is relatively easy. The major challenge with plug tackle lies in learning how to use it habitually and effectively as a casting tool. Because of the revolving spool operation, casts into the wind with lighter lures run the risk of creating "backlashes" or "bird's nests" on your reel. This challenge still exists despite advancements in the backlash control adjustments of plug reels. The best way to be a plug-casting master is constant practice at thumbing your spool throughout your cast after setting the appropriate spool and backlash control settings on your reel.

Fly tackle is a study in contrasts. It provides the angler the greatest combination of satisfaction and sheer frustration of all tackle options. It is ten times harder and ten times more fun. It lowers productivity and raises self-esteem in the same day. It will bring out your most colorful epithets and your biggest smiles. Speed is your ally in the enticement of the bite; however, speed and fly fishing generally do not go together. When you employ the usual long, heavy, and bulky needlefish fly, things can get challenging. To compensate, your fly rod must be at least nine feet and you must cast as far as you can.

Speed can be achieved by extremely fast stripping or placing the butt of the rod between your knees and stripping with both hands.

This latter technique, however, creates a difficult hook-setting dilemma. The good news is that if you find the long-cast, fast-stripping technique difficult or unproductive, other options can be used with fly tackle. Smaller, deceiver-like flies with lots of flash also work with a twitch and strip retrieve. Poppers can be retrieved the same way, sometimes causing explosive strikes!

As with any other fishing tackle, with fly tackle you get what you pay for. However, do not be fooled into thinking you must spend a thousand dollars for a good fly outfit. It is true that how long it lasts will depend on the cost, but for the average angler, a reasonably priced starter outfit should be around $250. Look for fly rods with what is called "high modulus." This is an engineering materials term that simply refers to the stiffness or fastness of the rod: the higher the modulus, the stiffer the rod. The higher the modulus, the easier it will be to cast, giving less vibration or lost energy. This translates to more energy going into the cast.

The sky is the limit when it comes to fly reel prices. The most important fly reel features are a smooth drag, large line capacity, and excellent corrosion resistance. Fly reels that hold at least two hundred yards of backing plus the line are preferable for those trophy barracuda you will have to motor after. Anodized aluminum construction, whether machined or assembled, are preferable over painted or powder coated. The difference in corrosion resistance of various fly reels is staggering—pay careful attention! For barracuda on the flats, it is a great advantage to select a reel with as large a diameter or arbor as possible. This, of course, will greatly assist in the retrieval rate. Every additional inch of diameter yields an additional three inches of line retrieval per turn, and your trophy will be released with a shorter battle time, which greatly increases its chances of survival.

Line Choices

Mono and braid both have their place in effective barracuda fishing. Mono is best for spin casting lures. Although mono creates some line twist problems, for some reason the small-diameter braids create nasty tangles in spinning reels with repetitive casting of surface lures. The nature of surface barracuda lures is that they ride on top most of the time. This technique is usually performed with the rod tip straight up in the air, which promotes the best speedy skipping effect. The unwary spin fisherman may not notice that the braided line is coming in loosely and may not remember to tighten it periodically.

Tightening braided line is easily accomplished by making a long downwind cast and reeling in with one hand forward of the reel, holding the braided line and tightening it on the spool as it comes in. Most of the time, if you forget, you end up cutting off a lot of valuable braided line. You will not have this problem if you remember to wind on tight-braided line from time to time. Monofilament nylon has the advantage of not forming such tangles when spin fishing a skipping, surface barracuda lure.

Microbraid line excels in three areas. First, it has very good abrasion resistance. Second, it never gets line twist. Third, it has more hook-setting efficiency than mono. If you pull back on your rod twelve inches to strike your 'cuda, your braided line will also move twelve inches back to you. Mono's inherent stretch does not allow for such deliberate, powerful strikes.

Braid is definitely an advantage in 'cuda fishing in sea fan–laden oceanside flats. Many a catch has been saved from the line parting by the braid's ability to hold together while wrapped around numerous obstacles. Because it does not fray like mono, braid lasts at least ten times longer. If the truth be told, with careful use you may not have to change your line for a year or more. It is here that the economy of braid versus mono comes shining through.

Line twist on spinning reels is a thing of the past with braided line. If the angler is a little over-excited and cannot stop reeling even when the 'cuda is all the way to the tip top, never fear. This is why spinning reels are the best application for braids. The high retrieval rate of a spinning reel with no line twist is a beautiful thing.

Braids are excellent for setting the hook, but the real reason braids have made such an impact is they are simply lower maintenance because of fewer spool changes. For catching giant 'cudas on the flats, they are a real advantage—especially when it is springtime and you can catch a dozen twenty-five-pounders in an hour.

Pound Class Selection

Selecting the right line class depends on the goals of the angler: some anglers like the greatest challenge and some anglers like the greatest chance to land the fish. If your target is five- to fifteen-pound barracuda on spinning tackle, ten-pound line class is just right because it allows the bigger ones to run far and "scream" the reel—but with a reasonable chance of landing the fish. For the smaller barracuda under five pounds, four- or six-pound line class is really enjoyable. Finally, if you are targeting the larger barracuda on the flats—twenty- to forty-pounders—on spinning tackle, fifteen- to twenty-pound line class is adequate. With the use of braids, however, sometimes the line test is higher than needed. With the smaller diameter braids, line selection is based on workability of the line or matching the line diameter to the rod and reel combination. Consider it a safety factor.

Plug tackle line selection follows the same parameters; however, with light plug tackle, be wary of "overlining" the reel. Light plug reels sometimes are not made for the long screaming runs of a big 'cuda. This vulnerability, coupled with using a heavy test line, can cause a plug reel to seize up before the day is through. Unless the reel is a fairly heavy-duty saltwater model, light line selection in six- to ten-pound is best.

Fly tackle tippet strength selection is purely a question of the "sport" of it. The angler who has caught many large barracuda on the flats may want to choose a ten-pound test tippet. If the angler is a novice to this specialty, a "beginner-friendly" tippet may be constructed by simply running the twenty-pound butt section straight to the bite tippet. This latter rig catches lots of fish with little maintenance.

The Best Times of the Year for Barracuda

Springtime is definitely one of the best times for big 'cudas on the flats. During the spring mullet run in April, gangs of big barracuda are on the prowl in the shallows. You will often see mullet schools on the flats "showering" away from barracudas. The 'cudas will be poised in stealth-and-ambush mode on every piece of structure on the flats. This will happen again during the fall finger mullet run on the flats of Miami's Biscayne Bay. If you have an electric motor on your flats boat,

A barracuda has vicious teeth that demand cautious handling. Photo by Scott Heywood/Angling Destinations.

As these anglers carefully pose this barracuda, it's easy to see why a wire bite tippet is always necessary. Photo by Scott Heywood/Angling Destinations.

consider trolling a mullet to attract a trophy barracuda, but be sure to troll in at least two feet of water.

In the wintertime, barracuda may remain on the flats longer than the other flats species from Miami to Key West, but they will ultimately leave those flats when the surface water temperature drops below sixty-nine degrees. When the temperatures drop into the low sixties, any 'cuda you find on the flats tend to be more reticent about striking.

During the heat of the summer months, barracuda tolerate the heat long after the bonefish drop off into the channels to find cooler water. Therefore, his majesty will be a great source of entertainment on South Florida's flats during summer and for the better part of the year. On the most sweltering summer days from Miami to Key West, barracuda may be all that you will find in your shallow water explorations, and they will provide welcome action. Summer 'cudas may be smaller than the offshore giants that come to the flats for mullet in spring and fall, but the modesty of their size can be offset by utilizing ultralight tackle.

Effects of Moon Phase and Tides

The effect of moon phase on flats barracuda is very simple: moon phase affects the depth of the water column. During the new and full moons, the flats feature higher high tides and lower low tides. Additionally, the spring tides produce high water in the morning. Experienced flats fishermen know that flats barracuda are structure-oriented and love shorelines and rock piles on the flats; therefore, more water depth early in the morning will produce more fish on that structure. This enhanced spring tide effect often means that morning bites are usually better because you know where the fish are and you are well positioned for your angling efforts on the flats. All fishing spots are affected differently by tide, but by and large, flood (incoming) tides produce the best big 'cuda action. The neap tides produce the opposite effect: low water in the morning. This keeps the fish from rising on the structures or flats until midday or later, which may not be as productive.

As the tide falls, the barracuda have no choice but to leave the crown of the flats and retreat to the deeper sections or the channel, thus making them a little harder to find. The lower the tide stage, the deeper and more concealed they go.

The poling depth of water you want to be working is the same as that normally associated with mudding bonefish and cruising permit, which is generally three to five feet of water. Do not spend too much time looking in very shallow water, unless you are looking for the smaller fish.

Poling Strategies

If you spot a barracuda while poling the flats, do not underestimate the caution of this fish and its tendency to spook in its own fashion. Unlike bonefish, which bolt away if they see you, barracuda may go into caution mode by standing their ground. Their spooked state is evidenced by their unwillingness to strike your presentation. Perhaps they are territorial and stake a claim to a piece of flats real estate they are not willing to give up. What is vital in your poling technique is that you learn to be quiet and make your skiff and yourself as invisible and unobtrusive as possible. Remember you are hunting; stealth should be your poling motto. Whether you are after bonefish or barracuda, you are the intruder in their domain.

When flats fish see a boat coming at them or "feel" it in their lateral line, it is likely they sense that you are bigger than they are and that you represent a threat to their survival. Never step around on the boat. I cannot count the number of casts that have been ruined because the angler wanted to move for a better shot. If you must, simply rotate your torso and do not move your feet. Lessen the impact of your pushpole foot on the bottom. This may mean slowing it down as it descends, especially if you are on hard rocky bottom that 'cudas may favor. It also may mean changing ends and poling with the point end. Try to eliminate hull slap. This problem has all but gone away in the newer skiffs, but it never hurts to be aware of it. Rotate and position your poled boat so that the wind-driven waves are not at the bow. Good poling techniques are essential for optimal results on the flats.

Advice on Live Bait, Lures, and Fly Selections

Barracuda willingly strike almost any live bait, provided it is properly rigged and presented. To attain that goal, stick to the following parameters. Leader length should be as short as possible, but long enough to avoid cutoffs. Barracuda will likely avoid obviously unnatural terminal rigs, so limit your wire leader and hook to the most subtle but workable sizes. Never let your wire leader length be less than twice the length of the bait. While slow trolling or pitching your live bait, the flight response the bait goes through is dramatic. When the live bait senses a 'cuda about to strike, its lateral line goes into total alarm and chances are the bait will come flying back to the protection of the boat. Keep up with it by cranking your reel to keep the slack out of your line. Otherwise, the bait will run up ahead of the leader. During the violence of the pursuit, the predator may cut the mono section of the leader or the line as it strikes at the bait. Too heavy a leader will detract from the bait's action. Number five through number seven wire is the best for the range of conditions for barracuda on the flats.

Barracuda lures are among the simplest of lures. It is the action that is the challenging part. The most successful lure ever made for barracuda is simply a piece of colored rubber tube with a wire leader run through it and a treble hook coming out the far end. The challenges are the arm-blasting, warp-speed retrieves you will employ each day. Barracuda love to strike many other lures on the flats. Shiny, lipped swimming plugs or long, soft baits that zoom along work quite well. My all-time favorite is the SeaBee—a shiny, lipped plug with the lip removed. It is quite different from all other plugs because the profile is flat. When retrieved, it tends to slap the water just like a needlefish. It is one of the best plugs ever made, and the 'cudas seem unable to resist it.

I am not a big fan of the traditional super-fast stripping technique for fly casting to 'cuda. In most cases, you can entice and catch flats 'cuda on any number of fly patterns with a little flash. The trick to retrieving flies for following barracuda is to make the predators' curiosity get the better of them. Strip your fly back to your rod tip in a twitchlike manner. Keep your eyes glued on the fish and watch the fish's response to your strip. The dance step should be pause, twitch, long strip, and repeat. Your enemy in your fly fishing retrieve is luring the fish too close to the boat before it strikes the fly. Keep the fish as far away from the boat as possible while you fool it into making the bite.

As far as hooks are concerned, I prefer the Owner Aki hook for live bait. I lightly sharpen only the tip of the hook with a diamond hone. This yields an incredibly effective hooking weapon. For flats 'cuda, try using an extra long shank 3/0 hook if you use live shrimp. This rig is equally good for permit and bones, and no wire leader is required. If you do not have an extra long shank hook, try rigging two hooks: put the point of the hook (which is already tied onto the leader or Bimini Twist) into the eye of another hook. Then put the shrimp on the added-on hook. This, in effect, makes an ultralong shank hook.

Lure and Bait Placement Strategies

A flats 'cuda is a wary, yet curious, character. When you spot a nice 'cuda, it is not necessary or even strategic to cast directly to the fish or in the path of the fish. Unlike bonefish, which often feed by picking up the scent trail, barracuda can easily see or hear the landing of a presentation in a full 180-degree periphery. You can cast your bait well to one side of your quarry. You might try as far away as fifty feet or more, and let the barracuda's curiosity about the sound of your presentation work to your advantage—their hearing is incredible. If the fish does not respond, try the next cast a little closer. Your overall placement strategy for 'cuda on the flats is to entice a strike before the fish sees you or your skiff and turns away in a state of alarm or caution. As ambush predators, they will interpret too close a cast as an attack upon them. In contrast, if they spot anything in flight away from them or to one side, they will interpret this as a feeding opportunity.

Fighting Strategies

First, when the fish surges or runs, lower your rod tip a bit to take the initial line pressure off the rod guides. As soon as the run stops, raise the rod higher again. Second, raise the rod even higher above your head in areas of rough terrain, like the usual expanses of sea fans on the outside of the Atlantic oceanside flats. Third, "bow" to a larger barracuda when it goes airborne—you don't want to lose your thirty-pounder because the hook pulled when he landed. Finally, when the fish is close to the boat, give it the "down and dirty." If it runs to the left, you pull to the right. If it runs to the right, you pull to the left. If the last few rounds of the battle with a trophy 'cuda occur in obstruction-free water, put the rod down low to the water, hold the spool when you sense the fish is weakened, pull judiciously for victory, snap some photos, and make a quick release!

Flats Hot Spot: Best Areas on the Flats for Barracuda

The great barracuda is a structure fisherman's delight. For an excellent shallow water reference point, focus on things we can see, such as islands, reefs, wrecks, channels, and rock piles. South Florida, from Miami to Key West, offers a seemingly never-ending supply of this terrain. Start with the nearest island and approach it at the higher tide stages. Fish the flats all the way around it until you find where the fish like to hide. If you are fishing with live bait, slow troll along the flats edges and the channels that grace the island.

The aforementioned rock piles on the oceanside flats from Soldier's Key to Elliot Key create structure-oriented habitat that barracuda simply love. While permit flit in and out of the rocks for a crunchy or spiny snack, his majesty Snaggletooth uses the crevices and shadows of that very same structure for a hide-and-pounce feeding strategy to take passing finfish like blue runners, balao, mullet and needlefish. Your strategy will be to stake out a reasonable distance from these hot spots on either "side" of the high tide and toss the baits and lures so thoroughly discussed in this chapter by Captain Jon.

11

Snook

With
Captain Butch Constable

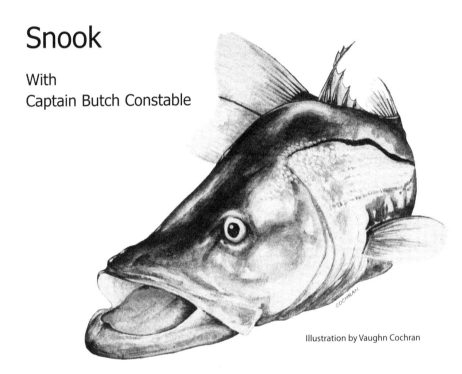

Illustration by Vaughn Cochran

Snook (*Centropomus undecimalis*)

Size Range: 5 to 40 pounds

Florida State Record: 44 pounds, 3 ounces

Florida Habitat: Passes, cuts, grassflats, and brackish mangrove canals of southern Florida

Baits: Live shrimp, mullet, pinfish, jigs, plugs, and flies

Tackle: 10- to 12-pound spinning and baitcasting; 10–weight fly

Snook Hot Spots: Large snook over twenty pounds swim the beautiful grassy shallows of the Indian River Lagoon network.

Fishing for Snook, by Captain Butch Constable

Part of the life history of snook is that they grow up in shallow fresh water inshore. At that point they are little tiny fish, up to about a foot long, that you hardly ever see: they hide in seagrass, docks, or mangroves. As they get larger and become "teenage" fish, they migrate down toward the grassflats—the intermediate ground. These fish are big enough to fend off predators and big enough to venture out more, just like teenagers reaching the age when they want to get going. Then they become mature spawning fish that typically run over twenty-six or thirty inches. These are the snook we see in large schools congregated in the passes, inlets, and along beaches. Putting matters in habitat perspective, the big spawners are on one end in the inlets, and the little fish are on the other end upriver. In between are the teenage fish that are sixteen to eighteen inches long, up to perhaps thirty inches. They are the most mobile group of snook and you will find them in a broader area than the other two groups. While the teenage snook are the ones you will be targeting on the flats, you will still see some way upriver, some on the beaches, and some in the inlets with the bigger fish. But predominantly, those are the fish you will see in the middle grounds between the fresh water and the ocean.

The optimal middle grounds on Florida's east coast are the Indian River flats from Stuart northward, and in Jupiter's shallow shorelines. Florida's west coast has extremely large areas of middle ground flats, like Pine Island Sound and Charlotte Harbor.

Prospecting for Snook on the Flats

When you want to explore a new Florida flat for snook, be sure to start your explorations on a calm day. A calm day gives you three things: clear water to see cruising snook, the ability to see bait schools dimpling on the surface, and the capacity to see any wakes that the snook are pushing. Another big key is to explore the flat on a full low tide and a full high tide, at least the first couple of times, to investigate. During a full low tide, it will become quite obvious where the potholes, deeper channels, and cuts are located. The low tide lets you map out where you will find the "holding" stations into which the snook fall back as the tide drops. Interestingly, some of these potholes, channels, and cuts still have snook in them during the high tide, because these spots on the flat offer excellent ambush and safety zones for the snook. Conversely, the parts of the flat that are out of the water on the low tide may hold snook only on the highest stage of the tide. Your explorations should include the low tide flat during narrower tidal fluctuations of a quarter moon, and the extreme spring low tides of the full and new moons. A low spring tide will help reveal even more of the bottom features.

Explore the flat during high tide so that you can access areas where you could not go on the low tide. When you are fishing Florida's flats during a full low tide, you may see a fish way off in the shallows but you cannot get to it. A full high tide provides more access to the places on the flat. During a full high tide you might see bait schools on top of the potholes and small cuts you observed during the full low tide. These spots may turn out to be highly productive for flats snook.

Snook Habits and Fishing Tactics

One thing to remember is that snook, like many fish, have a comfort zone as far as water depth is concerned. Even when you encounter snook in shallow flats water, you can bet there is deep water nearby— like a hole or a channel—that they can drop into when they get spooked. Another crucial clue appears when you are running along a channel or across the flat at high tide and you see a bunch of snook taking off. Pay attention to which direction they are going to find their sanctuaries.

If you run around a mangrove point at high tide and spook some snook that were higher in the water column, you might see them run off and then move to an adjacent spot on the flat that is deeper. This sanctuary might be an area for them to hide during any phase of the tide but especially when they are cautious or in a low tide mode. Even if you saw the snook higher in the water column at the top of the tide, when you go by at low tide you will no longer see them because they are on the bottom. Be careful and assume they might still be in their grassflat sanctuary. When fishing for flats snook in these situations, I either put a live bait on the bottom or use a crank bait or a jig and bounce it on the bottom in an area where I cannot see them. It momentarily turns sight fishing into basically an educated guess.

When the tide is up, snook seek spots such as structures and contours where they can hide and await ambush feeding opportunities. The simplest examples of a structure might be a blown-down tree or some fish-house pilings on the high tide flats of Pine Island Sound. Other contour variations, such as potholes, can also hold snook. Carefully search flats edges for sharp drop-offs that come up to the flat. In Stuart, you can actually anchor near the potholes and wait for the snook to come into them on an ebb tide when the water gets too shallow elsewhere on the flat.

Snook are primarily night feeders, so if you get out very early in the morning you will see more and catch more. After the sun comes up, these fish often drift down into a hole and take the day off—then later they will come back out. Flats snook may stay out longer on cloudy or rainy days, but generally when the sun starts coming out, they start turning off—it's just the way they are.

Hunting Strategies with Your Flats Boats

Early morning on the grassflats is the time to watch for bird signs and snook pushing water; however, if you are really trying to hunt snook

Baitcasting or plug reels work well on snook that are close to solid structure. Photo by Bass Pro Shops.

Early morning yielded a whopper snook for Jim Porter off a beach flat. Photo by Jan Maizler.

along the bottom, you should do that later in the day. Late morning to midday is an excellent time to familiarize yourself with new flats as you hunt for flats snook. Obviously, the middle of the day at low tide would be the best time span. This gives you the best overhead light and through-water visibility, so that you will not disturb as many fish. As far as timing goes, I recommend going out first thing in the morning when you have a half-outgoing tide at daylight. When the tide drops to low tide, look around. With the sun up, you can see everything.

As you explore and hunt snook, propel your skiff by using an electric trolling motor or by poling—do not run the outboard motor. You want to move slowly and look, not only for obvious snook and baitfish schools but also for everything else you could possibly imagine might be relevant for snook hunting on the Florida grassflats. Remember to think outside the box.

Captain Jeff Smith prepares to net some live bait for snook on the flats. Photo by Jan Maizler.

Whether you are on the pole or the electric motor, a stealth approach is dictated by the circumstances of where you are on the flat and what you need. Generally, I use either a pushpole or an electric motor. Sometimes I use both at the same time—I put the trolling motor on and then use the pole as secondary propulsion, especially in strong wind and current situations. In most situations the trolling motor does not spook the snook if you run it slowly. It is especially nice when you need to cross a channel without getting the big motor running.

"Transition" Snook Fishing

When the summer spawning season begins to come to an end and the bigger snook have spawned in Jupiter inlet or Stuart, these fish may work their way offshore. Otherwise, they are working their way inside. A legitimate question is whether these "transition" fish sometimes cross the flats during their travels inland. I do not see many on the flats themselves. There are some bigger transition fish on the flats but not as many as in the inlets. For instance, in Stuart inlet, where perhaps a couple of thousand fish were spawning and they start to move inshore, you can hardly follow their movements by just fishing the flats. I believe this is primarily because they travel in the deeper water in the channels. Unless you are fishing the channels with bigger baits, I think you are less likely to catch them. One significant exception to this is during the fall mullet and baitfish run along the Treasure Coast and Gold Coast. I have seen some truly huge transition snook come rushing out of the channels to crash and pursue the finger and larger mullet on the flats at this time of year. Snook are opportunistic feeders that cannot resist this type of feeding situation. In my experience, the most consistent size snook present on the flats are the teenagers.

Snook Season and Water Temperatures

The approximate season for flats snook from Tampa to the Keys all the way up to the Indian River is related to the Florida location, time of year, and water temperature. In my experience, the snook season is shorter on the east coast than it is on the west coast. The fishery on the west coast starts much sooner. I have been to the Chokoloskee area all the way up to Charlotte Harbor, and in some habitats snook can be caught during most of the year, except perhaps the very coldest times. The Treasure Coast area is a smaller habitat, and I would not start looking for snook on those flats until mid-April at the earliest, assuming warm weather. Generally, flats fishing for snook will run through October. The mullet run along the Treasure Coast spices things up on the flats before the season tapers off. The mullet that come across the flats excite the teenage snook that live there. You will see a lot of things going on in the flats—mullet schools with redfish, tarpon, jacks, and sharks in pursuit—everything sort of crowding them. The finger mullet schools even attract snook that normally stay in the channels.

Snook are tropical fish that like warm weather and water temperatures from the mid-seventies and up; however, some exceptions occur. For instance, in Florida Bay, you can sometimes catch snook in the potholes off Rankin Bight in slightly cooler weather. In addition, Jan Maizler told me he encountered lots of snook near Crocodile Dragover in very chilly weather. He said these fish suspend on top of mudflats trying to heat themselves up in the afternoon sun. Getting those fish to eat was another story, according to Jan.

For snook fishing in general, the warmer the water, the better. In the shallows of Jupiter, you will not see much until the water reaches about eighty degrees. On a milder stretch of weather in the wintertime, you might encounter windless conditions in which the shallow water will warm up from seventy-four degrees on an early morning flat to eighty degrees by midday.

Regarding flats fishing for snook in the "bottom half" of Florida, watch for water temperature even if is not the snook season. If you are snook fishing in the winter, sometimes it is better to go at midday or in the afternoon, after things have heated up. The opposite will hold true in the summer. The snook will be sitting on the deeper bottom during the hottest midday times, so you have to go at daylight or earlier.

Snook Weather

Snook are the most notoriously cold weather–vulnerable of Florida's flats fish species. In Florida, snook fishing season is closed during most of the months of December and January because the snook are too vulnerable to the cold weather; the cold-stunned snook on the surface are too easy prey. Snook do fine in warm weather because it is in their tropical genetic makeup to do so. When the cold winds of the fall and winter fronts cross the flats of central to southern Florida, snook head for the comparative warmth of the adjoining basins and channels. A slow-moving front of mild duration is more benign, while a fast-moving front of extremely cold air that lasts for five to seven days is most dangerous to a snook. A snook caught in comparatively shallow water in this latter type of front may die. Fortunately Florida's diverse marine environment affords most snook some cold weather respite.

Casting Strategies

The first thing to remember about the feeding habits of flats snook is they are hide-and-strike feeders. This is in contrast to the bottom-feeding behavior of bonefish and redfish. Flats fishing for snook is not based on sight casting to the fish themselves but rather on "probe" casting to likely places in very shallow water. Potholes on the flats, blown-down trees, mangrove points, and any other possible structures that serve as ambush stations all deserve careful casting. Contrary to the usual practice, cast your offering as far away from the honeyhole as possible, yet close enough to elicit the snook to follow it out from their lair and strike it. This method keeps your hooked snook from spooking out other snook that may be hiding in that same target area.

If you want to catch the maximum number of snook hiding in a potential hot spot, make it your practice to make them come out. It is also a good idea to try to catch them without chumming to see how aggressive they are. When you are casting artificial lures, cast a good distance away from them on your first cast. If you don't get any strikes, then start working in closer and closer and see if a fish or two will come out. The worst thing you can do is cast your lure on top of them; they are not accustomed to having their bait attack them, and they will spook off in this shallow water.

I make my first cast approximately twenty or thirty feet away and use a surface lure that makes a little noise. I always work the lures rather slowly at first, to get their attention and coax one of the fish out of its hiding place. My first choice of surface plugs would be a dancing plug, a chugger, or a swishing plug. If there is no strike, I choose a lipped swimming plug that works deeper in the water column and will attract snook that are less aggressive or closer to the bottom.

Another variation is to precede your plug casting by tossing in some hors d'oeuvres like whitebait. Using the same principle as with the live chum, I try to throw the baits away from the hole. When you throw three or four baits in there, one of them will probably swim back toward the hole. If that particular bait gets chased or struck at by a snook, I throw a plug right behind it. This method is one of the most effective and visually pleasing tactics, and most important, you are not dumping your initial probe casts right on top of hiding snook.

Some of the likelier places at which to probe cast are points with mangroves or downed Australian pines with current flowing around them. It seems the trees out in the middle of the flats do not have as many snook, so pay particular attention when these structures are against deeper water, such as holes and channels. If you add the natural presence of minnows or whitebait to these features, you are close to an ideal flats fishing scenario for snook.

Artificial Lure Strategies on the Flats

Artificial lures—including flies—are available for every snook situation on the flats. Consider all the polarities that technology offers us when choosing lures for flats snook.

- Hard-bodied lures versus soft, fleshy lures
- Scented lures versus unscented lures
- Surface lures versus suspension baits versus bottom-bouncing lures
- Light lures versus dark lures
- Lifelike replica lures versus creative lures
- Lures with built-in action versus lures that require rod activity
- Noise-creating lures versus quiet lures

Be sure to stock your tackle box with all the lures you will need for all the different snook conditions. Start by experimenting with various artificials—if you don't get action on the lure that you are using, change your lure based on the categories listed.

You might start with a hard-bodied, light-colored plug that chugs along the surface. You toss it over a flats pothole, but get no strikes. Your next choice should be a different category of lure—perhaps a swimming, lipped plastic plug that looks like a finger mullet. Cast that offering over the pothole and the deeper retrieve with a flashy finish on the plug may just do the trick. If not, perhaps choose a dark, bottom-bouncing, soft-bodied shrimp replica lure. Above all, experiment with artificial lures until you find one they are striking that day. Do not limit your offerings to your favorite lure—perhaps another lure will catch three times the amount of snook.

Many anglers always use the same retrieve with their lure. For maximum success with flats snook, you need to vary the retrieve, especially if you are sight fishing. If it is a surface plug, start by making it splash a lot briefly; then slow it down to get their attention, and go slow until they get up to it. Then speed up your lure a bit to convince your snook that the bait is fleeing—it must pounce on your offering if it is to catch up in time.

Particularly with a fly, do not strip it too fast until the snook starts coming after it; then pick up the speed and move it. Do not spook the fish; just splatter the fly a little to get the quarry's attention. The basic idea with all artificials or flies is to match your retrieve with the visible activity of the fish in pursuit. Watch its response to what you are doing to see which actions are working.

The use of a clinch knot versus a loop knot has always been a topic of debate when using artificial lures. I have tried to determine whether it makes a difference, and in some cases it does! If you are using Clouser-type flies, dancing plugs, or bottom-bouncing jigs, a loop knot is appropriate. With other artificials, I do not use loops; I usually just tie a regular tight knot. That is just a personal preference, but one that is founded on a lot of experience. In addition, some lures—particularly surface plugs—are already outfitted with a split ring that will give you the freedom of a loop knot.

My current standby lures are YoZuri Crystal Minnows and the DOA TerrorEyz, Bait Buster, and shrimp. For snook on fly, we designed a few patterns. I really like two of them. One is basically an anchovy pattern. It looks like a little minnow or baby pilchard. The other, named Butch's Baby, is like a Seducer pattern with a leaded eye on it. This makes the latter fly a bit like a bucktail lure that bounces a little when used with a sink tip fly line.

Snook Tackle

Heavy spin or fly tackle is not necessary out on the open flats. I use a spinning rod with eight-pound mono and I use a matching spinning rod with twenty-pound braided line, which has a comparable

Captain Mike Smith demonstrates the large gulping capacity of a snook. Photo by Jan Maizler.

diameter to eight-pound mono. The latter spinning outfit is for bigger snook or for fish that are close up against line-cutting structures like mangroves, trees, or rocks. A microbraid outfit is more than just an option—it is necessary equipment. I use a good three feet of fluorocarbon leader on my microbraid spinners, because I do not want the fish to see my running line.

When I am fly fishing for snook on the flats, I use a lot of clear sink tips. These lines work well when the water is a little deeper. Obviously, you need a floating line if the water is two feet or less. I use an eight-weight fly rod and a forty- or fifty-pound butt section. I put a piece of thirty-pound on it, which becomes the bite tippet. In still conditions, I might go down to twenty-pound and tie the fly onto that. Generally, I use only thirty- to forty-pound fluorocarbon leaders on flies or artificials.

Moon Phase and Tides for Snook

Moon phase is an important consideration when snook fishing on Florida's flats. As a rule, many guides prefer a new or full moon for snook fishing in Florida's shallows. This is because these lunar conditions feature the most water current and tidal activity. These spring tides dislodge more life forms to help the snook feed more vigorously on the flats. The weaker neap tides on the quarter moons tend to create sluggish feeding conditions. Without question, exceptions occur, depending on the individual locale and specific conditions.

Wading versus Boating for Snook on the Flats

With the exception of a few wading situations much farther north on the Indian River, flats fishing for snook is essentially a boat fishery, certainly in the sense that you need a boat to get there. If you are new to Florida's flats, I advise you to book a guide—not only is it necessary, but you will learn a great deal. I do that myself when I go to places with which I am not familiar. I call up a guide and try to get somebody to take me out, just as they might call me if they came to my area.

A limitation of wading is that it may leave you just out of reach of some action, because it is too deep to reach. A nice compromise between a full-fledged flats boat and wading are the car-topper kayaks. They are mobile, fairly stable, and well designed with storage in them. If you prefer wading, the kayaks are ideal because you can paddle somewhere and then get out and wade and pull it along behind you.

The snook flats of the Treasure Coast have hard bottoms, soft bottoms, or a combination of both types. Many of these flats are hard enough to walk on, which is good news for waders. If you plan to use

Captain Mike Smith holds up a darker backcountry snook with his angler. Photo by Jan Maizler.

a kayak to fish the flats for snook in this area, I advise fishing the falling tide all the way to dead low, as an arbitrary guideline. Avoid full high tide: at high tide the snook can go anywhere they want to go. As the tide drops, they are restricted to where they must go, and because a kayak floats in so little water, you can follow the snook as the tide ebbs and concentrates the fish.

Snook Fighting Techniques on the Flats

Two types of situations exist for battling a snook on the flats. First, you can fight a fish easily in plain open flats water—you simply finesse your snook by letting the fish run and thrash and tire itself out. The second situation is when you hook a snook against a structure. As your snook is running toward a dock, mangroves, or some other structure, put on as much pressure as you can. If the fish reaches the structure despite your efforts, immediately release the line pressure.

Generally, the fish will stop right where it is, because there is no reason for it to go into a line-cutting haven any longer: it feels safe.

Let's use a dock as an example. If your fish runs off the flat and under a nearby dock around a piling, release your line tension. As you ease your skiff up to the dock, keep your drag light and reel up slowly—and get ready. If the snook has one turn around the piling, put the tip of the rod down in the water, but keep the drag loose. Try to get down and pass your rod around the piling and back out; then tighten your drag and fight him with maximum pressure.

I have had many a big fish go under a dock and I run right up to it. It is swimming slowly near the piling. If it is not wrapped around that piling, I just keep winding very slowly. Finally, the fish moves away from the piling and I can pick the drag back up and catch it.

Flats Tip: Baitfish and Birds Offer Clues

Other important clues in hunting and fishing for Florida flats snook are two living features: baitfish and birds. Snook congregate and feed on baitfish aggregations on the flats. Sometimes bait like mullet or whitebait will not be visible, but the birds that feed on them always are. When you get to a flat, make bird-watching one of your first priorities.

Basically, I am concerned with three species: herons, pelicans, and terns. I am not as concerned with seagulls aloft or other types of wading birds below. The distribution of blue herons, pelicans, and terns can tell you a great deal, especially early in the morning. Often I take a bunch of photos, panning around for a 360-degree look with four photos, because you cannot remember everything. Then I have them in the camera for reference.

The birds are key clues everywhere, especially along the mangrove shorelines on the flats. For instance, while poling a flat, I may go around the bend of a mangrove shoreline and a couple of terns will be sitting there looking at something. Those birds are there because they sense feeding opportunities. Generally, they take advantage of predatory action or they are poised because they see the bait milling around. The birds have arrived because they are just picking on the baits, whether or not the snook are feeding, or because some snook or other fish have busted the water chasing bait and have gotten their attention. Often you will see the birds pick up and fly over to another spot on the flat and sit there. Those birds are sitting there for a reason, and it is worth taking a look.

Flats Hot Spot: Snook Hideaways

Around Sailfish Point in Stuart, Florida, you can find bunches of trees that have fallen into the water. If you choose the right conditions—a summertime weekday during an early morning high tide—you stand a good chance of catching a snook.

Flats Hot Spot: Easy Access to Snook

Florida beach flat snook are a flats fishing neophyte's dream—and summer is the time for its realization. Sanibel Island has ample beach parking for your vehicle. Simply cross over the sand dunes and work the stretch from behind the West Wind Inn all the way west to Bowman's Beach. This area is best on the rising tide or early and late in the day when there is less commotion from bathers. You will need a flats boat to reach the beach flat paradise of Keywadden Island, south of Naples. The lack of connecting causeways gives it less fishing pressure: simply pole your boat into the oceanside shallows and anchor your vessel a short distance offshore. For maximum stealth, hop out and walk the beach to experience supreme shallow water snook fishing in the bonefish manner and tradition!

12

Redfish

With Captain John Kumiski

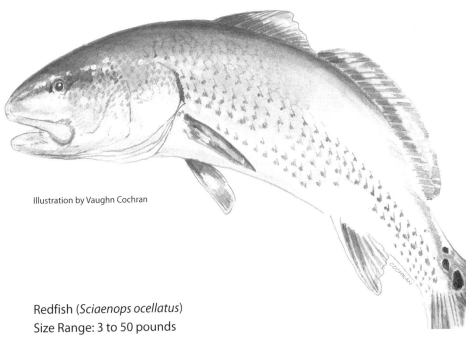

Illustration by Vaughn Cochran

Redfish (*Sciaenops ocellatus*)
Size Range: 3 to 50 pounds
Florida State Record: 52 pounds, 5 ounces
Florida Habitat: Passes, cuts, beaches, grassflats, and brackish mangrove
    shallows of Florida
Baits: Crabs, mullet, whitebait, jigs, spoons, plastic jerkbaits, and flies
Tackle: 10-pound spinning and baitcasting; 9–weight fly
Redfish Hot Spots: The Space Coast of Florida gets the nod as the trophy
    redfish epicenter, although the rest of the east-central coast of Florida
    can be excellent. Some of the top Space Coast waters are the flats of the
    Banana River.

Fishing for Redfish, by Captain John Kumiski

In our neck of the woods on Florida's Space Coast—the Mosquito Lagoon, Indian River Lagoon, and Banana River Lagoon—redfish keep more guides working and more boat companies in business than do any other fish. Properly called red drum, or *Sciaenops ocellatus*, they present magnificent sight fishing opportunities all year long, with fish ranging in size from little under-the-slot rats to forty-pound-plus bulls. Let's take a look at how and where to catch reds in these waters.

Tackle

Most local anglers use spinning tackle, with seven-foot, ten-pound outfits being most popular. Of course you will see a wide size range in use, and they will all work. Although some fishermen still like mono-

Redfish and bonefish love to grub around mangroves and other structure for crabs. Photo by Scott Heywood/Angling Destinations.

filament, more and more anglers are switching to braided lines due to all the advantages they offer. Regardless, a two- to four-foot-long leader of fifteen- or twenty-pound fluorocarbon should be attached at the business end of whatever type of line you use.

Casters who prefer plugging tackle should use equivalent tackle.

Fly fishermen should carry a seven- or eight-weight outfit; a nine-foot wand is most popular. Match the rod to a saltwater reel with at least one hundred yards of backing and a weight-forward floating line. I like to overline my rods by one line size in order to speed up fly delivery. Fly leaders should be a minimum of ten feet (longer is often better), tapered down to a twelve- or fifteen-pound fluorocarbon tippet, depending on time of year (lighter in winter) and size of fish targeted.

Fishing with Artificials

I think writing about lures is always risky, because if you ask ten good anglers what their favorite lures are you will usually get thirteen or fourteen different opinions. In spite of that, I will boldly continue.

Regardless of where you go, what you fish for, or what type of tackle you prefer to use, being able to cover the entire water column from top to bottom is vital to most angling success. You should have lures that float, lures that work the midrange depths, and lures that bump the bottom. We often fish in water less than a foot deep and seldom fish in water deeper than four feet, so covering the water column is not terribly difficult.

On the surface a popping or walk-the-dog type of plug is frequently good. Storm's Chug Bug or the Heddon Zara Spook are two examples among many other acceptable types. Keep in mind that during the late summer and into the fall, the abundance of floating grass makes using lures with gang hooks impractical.

Another single-hook lure that will fulfill the need for a surface bait is the DOA Shallow Running Bait Buster. This soft plastic mullet imitation will not hang nearly as much grass as a plug will and usually fishes every bit as effectively.

Bumping the bottom is easiest with a weedless jig. Both the Owner Bullet Type (#5146) and Sled Head (#5142) in the one-eighth-ounce size are wonderful for this. A wide variety of soft plastic tails can be used in conjunction with these jig heads, and even the manatee grass that carpets the bottom has a hard time sticking to them.

Three more lures will round out our slender kit. You must carry a one-fourth-ounce weedless spoon. Gold gets all the press but silver is just as effective. A variety of manufacturers produce these, and although my own favorite remains the venerable Johnson Minnow, use the one in which you have the most confidence.

The three-inch DOA Shrimp makes superior bait for sight fishing. With a Woodie's Rattle inserted, it becomes passable blind casting bait as well. Clear with gold glitter, night glow, chartreuse, and root beer are good colors to carry.

Finally, various soft plastic jerk baits are a must; you could probably leave all the other lures at home and get by with only these if you had to. They cast well, they are practically weedless, they can be rigged in a variety of ways so they are extremely versatile, and the fish eat them with gusto.

Fly fishermen can carry a small selection of flies, likewise keeping in mind that they need to cover the water column. Some Clouser Deep Minnows, some Bendbacks, some "minnow" patterns, some crab and shrimp patterns, a Rattle Rouser, a Spoonfly, and a few poppers, and you will be ready for anything.

Fishing with Bait

We can assume with reasonable certainty that the more of a fish's senses you appeal to, the more likely it is that the fish will take what you are offering. A live fish, shrimp, or crab in the proper size range appeals to a redfish's senses of sight (it can see the bait), smell (it smells the blood or juice from the bait), and feel (its lateral line picks up vibrations from the moving bait). If the redfish takes the bait into its mouth, then taste gets added to the mix. Bait is food, and it is effective for that reason.

Bait need not be alive to work. Dead shrimp, even frozen dead shrimp, are frequently just as effective as live ones. Dead crabs, even frozen dead crabs, even pieces of frozen dead crabs, are often effective. Chunks of baitfish, even if they have been frozen, work extremely well as redfish bait.

Anglers sometimes question me about using dead bait. My standard response is: "Think of it in terms of what you like to eat. Do you want to catch and kill the cow, or do you want it served hot and sizzling on a platter?" They immediately get my drift.

A redfish need do nothing more than open its mouth and inhale in order to take a dead bait. Most of the time they do not mind doing this. If you use a live mullet, especially if it is livelined, the fish has to chase it down and catch it. Frankly, much of the time they cannot be bothered. I rarely find mullet in the stomachs of redfish I fillet, and I check every single one that crosses the cleaning table.

Dead bait is effective and convenient for the fisherman. Anytime you get bait and then do not use it, you simply drop it into a Ziploc bag and put it into the freezer (check with your spouse first, obviously) for future use. When the mullet run in the fall, you can easily catch enough bait for several fishing trips—enough to get you through the winter months when mullet and other baitfish are scarce.

I stated that I check the stomach contents of every redfish I fillet. I have done this for years, and although I have not kept a log or anything like that, my generalized observations are as follows. About 25 percent of the time the fish are empty, with absolutely nothing in the stomach or intestines. When they have food in them, it is roughly 30 percent small fish, 30 percent shrimp, and 30 percent crabs.

Generally, the fish are more prevalent during the summer and fall, and the shrimp are more common in the winter and spring. Crabs of all types, including swimming crabs like the blue crabs and their relatives, mud crabs, small horseshoe crabs, spider crabs, and others, are evidently eaten whenever they are encountered.

The other 10 percent consists of oddities. I have found various types of marine worms in redfish stomachs. I cleaned one that had two sea horses in it. I cleaned one that had eaten a large giant water bug. One had a small American eel. I have cleaned several that had legs of large horseshoe crabs in them. If it looks like food and they are hungry, they will eat it.

Keep in mind that all the fish that I have looked inside have been legal, in-the-slot fish between eighteen and twenty-seven inches long, two to three years old. If you were to check in the stomachs of five-inch fish, or forty-inch fish, the situation might be different.

Types of Bait

For the purposes of our discussion, we are looking at three main classes of bait: shrimp, crabs, and baitfish. Let's take a look at the different types of bait and how to use them.

Shrimp

The easiest way to get this popular bait is to pick up a dozen or several dozen at the bait shop. Redfish definitely like to eat shrimp. So does every other type of fish in the lagoon system, including such species as stingrays, toadfish, catfish, pinfish, and puffers. These unwanted species will rob you blind, especially during the summer months.

I find shrimp most useful for sight fishing: that is, casting them into the path of fish that you can see. They are also widely used with a popping cork. You can use shrimp with a sliding egg sinker rig, but you will get pecked by pinfish, blowfish, catfish, stingrays, etc. One good thing about using live shrimp for bait is that the ones you have left over can be taken home and eaten. This is something you probably would not want to do with menhaden or worms.

Crabs

We have already noted that reds will eat all types of crabs with little if any hesitation. They make superb bait, especially for big redfish. The most commonly used bait crab for redfish is undoubtedly the blue crab, but any swimming crab you can catch will work. Large crabs can be cut into halves or quarters. Smaller, silver-dollar-sized live crabs make superb baits for big reds.

Live and frozen blue crabs are often available at bait shops. You can catch your own bait-sized blue crabs with a long handled, fine mesh dip net. Simply walk the shorelines of the lagoon and search for them.

Baitfish

In the Indian River Lagoon, three types of fish in four species make important bait sources for the redfisherman. Mullet, both black and silver, pinfish, and ladyfish all make superior baits. Other fish that can be used effectively include killifish (mud minnows), pigfish, mojarra, pilchards, and menhaden (pogies). We will concentrate on mullet, pinfish, and ladyfish. Anything you can do with them you can do with the other baitfish.

The silver mullet make excellent live bait for redfish. Blacks tend to be large and are usually steaked or filleted and used as chunk baits. Pinfish can be used live under a float or chunked. Because of their size, ladyfish are almost always chunked.

Wading or Boating?

The Merritt Island National Wildlife Refuge lies along the east side of the Indian River Lagoon across from and north of Titusville, and along the west side of the Mosquito Lagoon. Unimproved roads along the shorelines provide waders and hand-powered boaters miles of access. Unfortunately for waders, the bottom is soft enough to make wading a real workout. Nevertheless, when the fish are in, few ways of stalking fish are more effective than wading.

During the warmer months (mid-April through about the end of October) the only gear you need is some type of foot protection. Wading booties are the most practical. When it cools off, chest waders become a necessity for all but the hardiest anglers.

Hand-powered boaters can use kayaks or canoes effectively. You can launch these boats from loads of places. My best advice is to avoid skiff traffic and concentrate on places where the skiffs cannot go.

Anglers using powerboats will likewise find that a wide range of boats will get the job done. Johnboats, while somewhat noisy, can work well. Gheenoes and other types of small boats likewise work well, especially in better weather conditions. And of course the ubiquitous flats skiff was designed to operate in places like the Indian River Lagoon system with its extensive shallow grassflats.

Although some anglers use electric motors extensively, even while stalking fish, most boating fishermen find that a pushpole makes the best fish-stalking tool. This remains true whether you use a skiff or a canoe.

Now that you know what type of bait and tackle you need, and have decided whether you are wading or boating, let's look at the fish's behavior. Understanding how reds behave will help you catch more of them.

A well-outfitted flats boat like this one can help make your redfishing more successful. Photo by Ranger Boats.

Redfish Weather

Like our lovely little planet, the redfish go through a yearly cycle. Their cycle does not follow the calendar but rather the always changing length of daylight and ambient water temperature. The situation is a little different every year, because although the changing of length of day is a constant from year to year, the weather is not. Thus what follow are generalizations.

In the Indian River Lagoon, beginning in approximately November, the fish get into their winter mode. The adult fish, schooled up most of the time anyway, have finished spawning and stay mostly in the deeper basins (perfect weather days excepted), where they are hard to find. The juvenile fish, including those in the slot, tend to form schools at this time of year.

If the water temperature is dropping, the fish will be searching for thermal refuges and will be very hard to find. Days when fronts come through, or the day after a front, usually offer poor fishing for this and other reasons. If you luck out and find a hole full of fish, though, you will have a day you will never forget.

During sunny days when the water temperature starts to rise, the fish will immediately move into shallow water. Shallow water warms faster than deep water. The best fishing of the day will often be at sunset during the winter. The wind tends to lie down and the water has been warmed by the sun all day. Regardless of what the beginning water temperature is, if it rises three or four degrees, you will find feeding fish.

All of this assumes the wind is not howling. Redfish seem not to like the wind much. They like the same type of weather conditions we do: warm and sunny with little or no wind. It is not that they won't eat when it is windy, because sometimes they will. But they seem to prefer beautiful, warm, windless days.

Another factor to keep in mind while winter fishing is that fish are cold-blooded. I hear fishermen say, "They have to eat some time." Yes, they do. But during the winter, that time may not be today. Cold water slows their metabolism, so they do not have to eat as often. When they do eat, they seem to prefer smaller, lighter meals. Shrimp are great winter bait because they are easier to digest than baitfish. If you are flinging artificials, it might be a good idea to downsize. Smaller lures seem to work better during the cooler months.

Around April comes a discernible change in season. The patterns of the fish begin to change as the days lengthen and the water temperatures rise. Baitfish like silver mullet and pinfish start to appear. Good fishing can be an all-day-long affair. Sadly, this action only lasts a relatively short time—two or three weeks.

By the time mid-May arrives, the summer pattern is established. Those slot-sized fish, so plentiful and dependable during the winter, now become less predictable and harder to find. Prime fishing time frequently is over by the time the sea breeze kicks in. Let's look at a typical summer day on the lagoon system.

At dawn, a light breeze (zero to five miles per hour) comes out of the west. There may be a lot of activity in shallow water—tailing fish, showering bait, the welcome sounds of game fish feeding. As an angler, you certainly hope for this! Somewhere around 9:00 or 10:00

a.m. the air movement dies down and the water slicks out. It starts to get hot. Cumulus clouds start to build and make sight fishing difficult. Around 10:00 or 11:00 a.m. the breeze picks up, now out of the east as convection kicks in. This wind may quickly build to fifteen miles per hour. At some point rain starts to fall out of the now towering clouds, huge sparks start flying around, and the prudent angler gets off the water.

Many times I have watched a flat that was covered with fish in the morning go dead as soon as the sea breeze kicked in. Sometimes you can watch the fish swim to the edge of the flat and drop off into deeper water. Getting an early start during the summer is often a critical component of angling success.

Because of the usually stable and predictable summer weather, it is the best time of year to look for the schools of big, adult fish. They are frequently in shallow water, near the surface with their fins out of the water, very easy to see. Furthermore, as summer comes to an end the adults sometimes form huge spawning schools with hundreds of fish, a bonus find for any angler.

The other event that occurs at the end of the summer is the start of the annual mullet run. Silver mullet are tropical fish and cannot tolerate the colder water temperatures of winter. When the days shorten and the water temperatures begin to fall, they school up and head south by the billions.

The mullet run is a banquet for every game fish in the lagoon system, including redfish. The run typically peaks around the last two weeks of September and the first two weeks of October. Look for a mullet school with explosions occurring in it, and fish those. You might catch anything, but redfish certainly shadow mullet schools and will make up part of the catch.

After the mullet run ends, things quiet down a bit. Cold fronts start rolling through, and we're back into our winter pattern again. The earth has completed another cycle around the sun.

Redfish Behaviors

If you have ever lived with another person for any length of time, you come to a point in your relationship where you can easily sense their mood. After fishing for redfish for over twenty years, I have learned that they also have moods. They cannot give you a come hither or a look that could kill, like your spouse might give you, but their behavior gives you a strong clue as to how catchable they might be on any given day. Your goal as an angler is to observe and learn to interpret that behavior.

The fish have a limited range of behaviors. They might be lying in one place. They might be tailing very aggressively or much less so. They might be cruising at varying rates of speed. They might be pursuing bait. That is pretty much it.

A fish might be by itself, or it might be with one, or three, or a dozen, or fifty or more others of about the same size. Generally, all the fish in a group of any type behave in a similar fashion. The size of the group definitely affects their "catchability," for better or worse.

Let's examine the behaviors more closely. The hardest redfish to catch, and this is always true regardless of how many there are, lie motionless (or darn close to it) on the bottom. They are down deep, or as deep as they can be in a foot or two of water. These fish seem to lack all interest in eating. As far as I can tell (it is always your best guess, since the fish aren't talking), they just sit around looking for trouble. Since they focus their attention in the distance, they see you coming. They usually start swimming off before or during your cast. Simply showing them your lure is problematic.

The one rare exception to this is the fish that is asleep, and I have only found a few of these over the years. These fish (always singles) also lie motionless on the bottom, but they are completely oblivious to everything going on around them. If you put your lure right on the nose of such a fish you can sometimes wake it up. They usually spook off, but sometimes they just wolf down the lure. Sometimes they are so out of it that they respond to nothing until you poke them with your rod tip.

When Lady Luck smiles, you will find schools of fish that simply maintain their position, finning lazily high in the water column, apparently sunning themselves. A few individuals may have their fins poking through the water's surface into the air. Do not mistake these for tailing fish. They are finned-out fish, relaxed and happy. A good cast will usually garner a strike.

Redfish often cruise. Sometimes they follow a more or less circular route (usually single fish); sometimes they are apparently moving from point A to point B (singles to hundreds of fish). If you make it easy for them to take your offering by putting it directly in their path, they usually will take it.

The fish swimming in a circuit almost always take a well-presented fly or lure. When they swim in a circuit they are usually feeding on small minnows in shallow water. They come in, crash the minnows, swim back out some distance, turn around, swim in, and crash the minnows again. A good cast usually gets a strike.

On a couple of occasions I have had the good fortune of watching snowy egrets and redfish playing Pong (do you remember Pong, the first video game?) with mosquitofish (*Gambusia* minnows). The reds chase the minnows to the birds; the birds chase them back out to the fish; the fish chase them back to the birds; and so forth. These are circular route redfish at their finest!

I sometimes see redfish swimming in rough circles in sandy potholes in seagrass beds. These fish frequently roll on their sides and flash. Again, these relaxed, happy fish will almost always eat if you make a good cast. You can cast to the near side of the hole while they are on the far side and wait to move your fly or lure until they come back. You will almost always catch these fish.

Flashing is a wonderful behavior to see, because fish that flash are usually relaxed. When you find a large school, the flashes give you a good indication of their mood. Tense fish seldom flash. Flashing, relaxed fish usually eat well. Flashes are easy to see, allowing you to keep track of the school's location while they cruise.

All anglers love to find tailing fish. Tails tell you exactly where the fish are, and you know they are eating. What they are eating can sometimes be a problem when they are feeding selectively. Ordinarily, shrimp or crabs are the target item for tailing fish—easy enough to imitate. I have encountered redfish digging small brown marine worms out of the mud, and only a lucky fly choice that more or less matched the size and color of the worms finally turned the trick.

Redfish Behaviors: Other Considerations

Some days, if you bother the fish they just leave. When they are schooled, this is a heartbreaking event because you are unlikely to find singles (all the fish are in the school), and when they are gone, it's over. Other days they want to stay right where they are, and if you make them move they will circle like rabbits and within a few minutes come back to the same spot. You can (and should) keep fishing this same spot over and over until the fish finally wise up or it is time to leave. Again, their position in the water column gives you a good idea of how tolerant they might be. Up high is good.

Schools of fish offer great possibilities, and great hazards. A single fish works on its own—one pair of eyes, one pair of ears, one pair of lateral lines. If you spook it, it's gone, but this has relatively little effect on other fish that may be in the same area. A school works as a unit. One hundred fish mean two hundred eyes, two hundred ears, and two hundred lateral lines. If you spook one, they all spook.

Many anglers approach these schools much too aggressively. If you push too hard on the fish, they usually vacate the premises. A much better approach requires liberal doses of patience. Try to stay about fifty feet from the fish. They usually tolerate this quite well. Any decent saltwater fly fisherman ought to be able to make a fifty-foot cast with ease, and it is no problem with other types of tackle.

Instead of casting right into the middle of the school, work the fish on the edge, or better yet, cast the fly or lure to where they are going, and move it only after they get there. Take the time and trouble necessary to obtain the position from which you can get a good shot. Especially when fly fishing, casting from behind a school that is swimming away from you only serves to speed up their departure.

After the school of fish has decided to vacate, you can often follow them if you have an electric trolling motor. They usually move too fast for you to follow them with a pushpole. Stay far enough from the fish that they cannot tell you are there.

Redfish have notoriously short memories. Sometimes, after swimming a distance, they seem to forget why they are swimming so fast. They then slow down and start to relax. If this happens, immediately put the trolling motor up and approach them with the pushpole again.

I have followed schools for miles this way, and while it sometimes simply wastes time and effort, it pays off often enough that I try it every single time the opportunity arises.

Redfish Moods and Lure or Fly Selection

Sometimes a red will track your bait, evidently trying to make up its mind whether to take the bait or not. If you continue retrieving the bait you lead the fish right to you, and after it sees you it is not taking that bait, oh no! If you stop retrieving and the lure hovers in the water column, the red usually turns off. If the lure dives to the bottom, though, the reds often pick it right up. For this reason, I usually prefer using weighted flies when fly fishing for reds.

Weighted flies, especially those with dumbbell eyes, and almost all lures make a distinct plopping noise when they hit the water. Aggressive, feeding fish hear that plop and come looking for the groceries; however, nervous, spooky fish think the plop is death from above. The first couple of fish you throw to will let you know how they are feeling that day.

You can pretty much throw anything to hungry fish and they accommodate you. When fly fishing, fussy fish frequently require a nonweighted fly that comes down softly onto the water, like a #18 Adams parachute. I like Bendbacks or flash flies for this work, but other patterns will score, too. Let the behavior of the fish tell you what they want.

When spin fishing in this situation, cast the lure in front of and beyond the fish. Start reeling before the bait hits the water, keeping the rod tip high so the bait stays on the surface where you can see it. When it gets to where you would have liked to cast it if the fish were not so spooky, stop reeling and let it sink. The slightest twitch at that point is usually enough to turn the trick.

Keep in mind that some days the fish just won't hit lures. Some days they won't take bait, either. So when you find the fish being grouchy, just be happy you found some. I always prefer to find fish that won't eat than not to find fish at all!

Location, Location, Location

Newcomers to this area frequently find themselves overwhelmed by the amount of water available. Let's look at each lagoon separately, dividing them into sections to break the vast acreage of wet stuff down into manageable chunks.

The Indian River Lagoon

My book *Fishing Florida's Space Coast* has more detailed information on this entire area. In the Indian River Lagoon, the section from the NASA Causeway to the Max Brewer Causeway offers good fishing on the east side, most of which is in a manatee slow-speed zone. In this area, locally called the VAB flat, redfish of all sizes can be found all year long, although redfishing is probably best during the fall mullet run. When this area is good, you usually know fairly quickly. If you don't see anything in an hour or so, you should look elsewhere.

The next section north lies between the Max Brewer Causeway and the railroad trestle. The east side close to the boat ramp is used as a water sports area by jet-skiers and parasailers, and is best avoided. North of where they operate, the shoreline up to and including the causeway can produce fish, although I have never seen schools or big fish there. The west side of this section is a manatee slow-speed zone. It can fish well all the way from the little boat builder's harbor up to and including the railroad trestle.

North of the railroad trestle lies a redfish factory. On the west side the flat extends for miles, all the way to the north end of the lagoon. From singles to large schools, from smaller slot-size fish to jumbos, or maybe nothing at all, all will be encountered on this flat.

The same is true on the east side, which has more geography. If you want to catch fish there you must go on a search mission. Look for clean water and signs of life, then slow down and hunt for fish. If you don't find any within twenty or thirty minutes, try a different area.

I cannot offer any shortcuts besides putting in your time. Unless you fish this area every day, keeping track of where the fish are is a problem. Hunting them down is the solution.

The Mosquito Lagoon

You might find redfish anywhere in the Mosquito Lagoon, or you might not find any at all. Such is fishing.

You can divide this lagoon into two major sections—the southern "basin" section, from Oak Hill south to the southern terminus of the lagoon; and the northern "island" section, which runs north to New Smyrna Beach. Neither is necessarily superior to the other, but they fish differently.

The southern area has an open water basin with "deep" water. The average depth of the entire Indian River Lagoon system is three feet; in this basin it is five to six feet. This deep water basin is encircled by flats. If you are looking for the jumbo fish, this is the area in which to look.

On the east side are a series of naturally occurring islands. On the west side north of the Haulover Canal is the Intracoastal Waterway, with man-made spoil islands just to the west of the channel.

Again, you might find fish anywhere. Well-known areas that usually hold fish include the Middle Flat (also called the Whale Tail) at the south end of the lagoon; Tiger Shoal, east of Intracoastal Waterway marker 25; and Georges Bar, which runs east and west across the lagoon just south of Oak Hill.

North of Georges Bar is where the island section starts. A lot of fish congregate up there, but they tend not to be the jumbos. It is an intimidating area for the newcomer because few areas are marked, and navigation requires knowledge of the local area. It is a superior area for using canoes, kayaks, and other small boats, provided you have a chart or an aerial photograph that you know how to read, and a compass so that you know which way you are facing. After you learn your way around you can dispense with these items, but at first they are vital.

Again, there is a lot of water. Success requires the ability to hunt the fish down.

The Banana River Lagoon

The third and final lagoon in the system is the Banana River Lagoon. Physically, it is quite like the other two—a deeper basin ringed by flats.

An angler holds his fly in readiness for casting at a redfish. Photo by Scott Heywood/Angling Destinations.

It does not receive as much fishing pressure because it is not as pretty; most of the shorelines are completely developed. When the fishing is off in Banana River Lagoon, it is really off, but the converse is also true. And it holds a feature known and loved by anglers across the southeast—the no-motor zone of the Banana River Lagoon.

Being in possession of a motor—internal combustion or electric— is against the law in Banana River Lagoon. This greatly cuts down on the competition. The fish aren't buzzed by outboards all the time, so they tend to be more relaxed. Consequently, the no-motor zone offers some of the best redfishing in the state for those willing to trade sweat equity for fishing opportunities. This is a large, open-water area, not at all friendly to paddlers when the wind comes up. Keep that in mind before paddling six or eight miles into this stretch.

South of the no-motor zone the best fishing is in the section between SR 520 and the Pineda Causeway. This area has large manatee slow-speed zones and zealous officers patrolling them. The fishing, and the problem finding fish, is similar to that in the other lagoons. Again, the ability to hunt fish down is crucial.

For anglers with canoes and kayaks, the Thousand Islands area on the east side of the lagoon, inside of Cocoa Beach, provides a fine fishing area, mostly protected from the wind and motorboats.

This section of the Indian River Lagoon system offers world-class sight fishing for redfish. Although other places have more redfish and bigger redfish, no place else on the planet has the numbers of twenty- to forty-pound redfish available in two feet of clear water, sight fishable (with proper weather conditions) with fly or light tackle on any day of the year. Sometimes easy, frequently challenging, too often difficult and frustrating, the fishery here is special and unique. Give it a try and you will be hooked.

Flats Tip: Recommended Reading

This chapter by Captain John Kumiski is chock full of great directions to the world class redfishery along that part of Florida's coast that he calls home. His excellent book *Fishing Florida's Space Coast* provides a wealth of data for achieving success and maximal growth as a shallow water redfish angler.

13

Seatrout

Illustration by Vaughn Cochran

Seatrout (*Cynoscion nebulosis*)

Size Range: 2 to 12 pounds

Florida State Record: 17 pounds, 7 ounces

Florida Habitat: Grassflats and brackish mangrove shallows of Florida

Baits: Shrimp, pinfish, pigfish, whitebait, jigs, plastic jerkbaits, plugs, and flies

Tackle: 8-pound spinning and baitcasting; 8–weight fly

Seatrout Hot Spots: Huge spotted seatrout can be found in the east-central coast area of Florida—in places like Fort Pierce, Cocoa Beach, Titusville, and the Indian River. When it gets chilly, the deeper channels in North Biscayne Bay and the residential canals off the Indian River offer sanctuary.

You have gone to one of the best local tackle shops near the Indian River and were lucky enough to get the scoop about the current wading hot spot from the owner—your respectful courtesy paid off. The next morning before dawn you ease into the shallows from the roadside. You are cautious, yet you cannot stop your heart from beating in anticipation. Now, in knee-deep water, you wade along ever so quietly and listen for clues, because in this half-light your ears are as necessary as your eyes.

You think you hear—and then vaguely see—a few finger mullet shower. You quickly cast your surface plug alongside the periphery of this possible mirage. Before the plug lands, you feather the line to lessen the lure's impact in the calm water. Even if this moment is just a phantom tease, you take it seriously and ease the plug along in slow pulls. You can almost hear the swish of its tiny propeller blades. As your plug is within ten feet of you, you almost swear you see a bulge behind it. You stop the lure for a second, and then give it a sharp tug.

A moment later a huge splash engulfs your plug. You grab hold of your mind and resist immediately striking—waiting just a second more for your line to tighten and your rod to go down. Now is the time! With a flick of your wrist, you sink the well-sharpened hooks into the shadowy predator. Feeling the sting of the hooks, a big trout of about six pounds surfaces and thrashes in rage and alarm barely six feet from your rod tip. You struggle with your fish gingerly, knowing that too much pressure will tear the hooks out of its soft mouth tissues. A few more minutes of this dance ensue, and the trout's thrashes grow weaker.

It is time for the landing net. You slowly ease the fish toward the hoop's mouth, and finally it is in. You look down at your prize, its spotted beauty lighting up in the golden colors of the rising sun. As you release your trophy back into the lagoon, you are reminded of the feeling of oneness with both fish and environment that wading brings. Is wading for seatrout fun? You bet!

The seatrout is arguably the most popular Florida flats fish. At this time, the redfish appears to be a rival because its wide geographic distribution in the state, tendency to tail up, and larger size to about forty pounds have made it a more publicized species on the tourna-

The seatrout is one of Florida's most popular grassflats species. It is certainly one of the finest looking flats fish. Photo by Captain John Kumiski.

ment circuit. Yet I still contend that most anglers in Florida who fish our grassflats do so more often and more successfully for seatrout. Indeed, find grassflats and bays tied into brackish mangrove ecology in Florida, and you will likely find the spotted seatrout. They go by different names in Florida: spotsides, orangemouth, or speck. But regardless of what you call them, they are the same beautiful fish that grace the stringers, ice chests, livewells, and pans of grateful and admiring anglers.

Other factors that make them tops on the flats totem pole are the relative ease with which they can be caught and their superb flavor and edibility.

Seatrout are midsurface and surface strikers. They are not bottom grazers with underslung mouths like bonefish or redfish. The architecture of the seatrout's mouth features striking jaws and prominent single "snaggleteeth" above and below. This helps our predators grab and hold their prey before swallowing, not unlike an alligator but unlike the suction vortex created by striking snook and tarpon.

Seatrout Habits and Habitat

When targeting Florida's seatrout population, keep in mind that this species is often found in schools of smaller yet mature fish of one to three pounds. The larger fish of four to over ten pounds tend to be somewhat more solitary. Sometimes these two groups overlap—such as in mullet muds, finger mullet migrations, or shrimp hatches. An analogous situation might be kingfishing off Jupiter, Florida. Smaller kingfish schools are targeted in about one hundred feet of water off-shore, while the big "smokers" are fished inshore in about fifty feet of water with large live baits.

Distinguishing school trout from the larger, more solitary "gators" is a sound tactic because their feeding habits and locales vary. No doubt many flats anglers are quite aware of the enthusiastic feeding of smaller seatrout: find a school of them, and a large catch is probably assured. Often this occurs on a high tide grassflat with a popping cork and live shrimp. Big gator trout tend not to mix, and they frequent areas with higher ambush potential, like flats drop-offs, potholes, ex-tremely shallow flats that feature predawn mullet schools, and flats that have nighttime lights, docks, and boats alongside them. Gator trout are cautious, yet paradoxically are almost mean when they are intent on seizing and killing their prey.

In my long history as a self-proclaimed gator trout addict, I have examined many seatrout stomachs for their contents. Trying to deter-mine what constitutes preferred gator food, I have found needlefish, mullet, small seatrout, pinfish, pilchards, gobies, glass minnows, sea-horses, tiny snappers, pigfish, grunts, shrimp, and an occasional crab. It became clear to me that pursuing gator trout on the flats meant using larger finfish baits instead of the typical live shrimp rigs. My results have been excellent in the last forty years, with some of my trophy trout topping nine pounds. For Miami's Biscayne Bay, these are indeed large fish.

Flats Tip: Seatrout Bait

For large seatrout, forget about shrimp and small artificials. Stick with large finfish baits like live finger mullet, live "horse" pilchards, small live pigfish, or small live pinfish as your last choice. Barring live bait, try fresh mullet strips about six inches long or pinfish steaks or chunks. These larger live and dead baits are appealing to gator trout and are left alone by the ever-present pinfish schools. Large live shrimp simply do not last long enough on the flats to be found with regularity by huge seatrout. In addition, use lifelike larger swimming plugs that resemble finger mullet and large pilchards. You can use the larger artificial shrimp lures—such as the DOA—because these latter lures resist ripping apart by pinfish. Gator trout are somewhat like the stout yet affluent customers who frequent some cateries—a bit picky, but convincible when they are presented with a dish that is large, nourishing, tasty, and easy to eat.

Flats fishermen who target Florida seatrout seem to have less sunburn than anglers who pursue bonefish and permit. Sunblock aside, this is probably because seatrout anglers often get some of their best fishing in low-light situations: dawn, dusk, and cloudy days. Think about the winning combination of grassflats, low-light times, and big finfish or artificial baits.

It will be helpful for you to perceive the basic nature of this delightful fish by understanding not just what it is but what it is not. Seatrout join the snook and barracuda as "pikelike" flats fish that hide, ambush, and lunge-strike their prey. Again, seatrout can be extremely aggressive in the size of the baits they will seize for a meal. Like barracuda, seatrout rely on teeth and jaws to seize their prey on the flats. They do not possess the gill-flaring suction that snook and tarpon utilize. Seatrout tend to spread out on the Florida grassflats, while snook tend to stick together in groups in areas with tight cover, where current and ambush are the highlights. Seatrout, however, will take advantage of hidey holes like grass clumps and potholes. They simply do not cling to structures the way snook tend to do. In places like the grassflats of Florida Bay, Pine Island Sound, and Charlotte Harbor, you will often find both snook and redfish holding tight to the structure of mangrove root shadows and edges, yet the trout will be found away from the mangrove islands on the grassflat pastures.

Seatrout Habits, Distribution, and Time of Year

Your travels through Florida as an angler should keep you in the relatively constant companionship of spotsides, due to the species' wide distribution throughout the state. Florida is a perfect state for this fish, because it is a somewhat temperate, subtropical habitat. Good news indeed, because seatrout are one of the more temperate of Florida's flats fish.

Although seatrout can tolerate a variety of weather changes and seasonal variations, they can—and do—move into the moderate deeper channels when it gets too hot or too cold on the flats. These movement patterns make it possible to catch seatrout on or adjacent to the Florida flats all year long. This is another reason why this fish tops the totem of Florida flats popularity. Armed with knowing the low-light preferences and moderate temperature tastes of spotsides, it is almost axiomatic that your hunting on the grassflats during the heat of summer will be a dawn, dusk, or evening proposition. You can rest assured that plenty of big trout are on the prowl, swimming the predawn summer flats of Florida.

When fall brings jack-o-lanterns and later turkey and pumpkin pie our way, the days will be shorter with less sun time, and the water will be cooler. Seatrout fishing can be an all-day affair during this time of year. As the wheel of seasons turns toward winter, the coldest days feature seatrout on the deeper, warmer flats of six to eight feet, where they may hold on grass and mud bottoms instead of flats crowns of pure Thallasia or Cuban grass. As the afternoon sun warms the flats a bit more, especially on a falling tide, the trout may come into shallower water to eat forage species that are exiting the flat.

Winter afternoons offer good results—something Florida bonefishermen know all too well. During the coldest days of deep winter in Florida, while bonefish, tarpon, and permit anglers must sit home and daydream about their more tropical species, you might be out on the flats catching seatrout for a fine dinner that night! When the Great Spirit gives the wheel of seasons another turn and spring appears, the increasing warmth brings the trout by instinct and comfort back to the shallower grassflats—and again the fishery becomes an all-day affair.

It would be fair to say that seatrout spend the bulk of their life cycle in the grassy shallows. As youngsters, they hide in the same grassy recesses and forests that one day will become their own hunting grounds. Beginning as tiny fry, they feed on what they can and grow bigger as they rise to the top of the grassflats food chain to become King Trout. As grassflats predators, seatrout hunt the entire water column from top to bottom, yet they will not bottom-hunt in the grazing, grubbing way of bonefish and redfish. Rather, when trout are not on their usual midsurface to surface forays, they pursue baits like mullet strips that flutter to the bottom. In addition, they pounce down on bottom-bouncing bucktails—or better yet, soft weedless jerkbaits—that may resemble forage moving in the grassy bottom. Bonefish and redfish will suck in still-fished natural bottom bait, while seatrout prefer a bit of movement to the same type of bait.

Seatrout Weather Recap

Seatrout range much farther north than the tropical snook. Although they are among the "big three" mangrove brackish-water species, seatrout are found less often than redfish and snook under the protection of mangrove trees. More often, their preferred habitat is the open grassflats of about three to six feet often found in open bays. Like redfish, although the genetics of seatrout can bear cooler weather, the Florida strain of this species avoids the flats during bitter cold fronts. In contrast, seatrout are a little like bonefish in that their peak feeding seems to occur in the slightly cooler fall and spring, when the weather is more temperate. Above all, however, strong cold fronts drive seatrout off the grassflats.

Seatrout and Tide on the Grassflats

Due to Florida's position on our planet, the tidal range and variations of tidal levels are comparatively moderate. Naturally, during the spring tide times of the full and new moons, the tidal levels are more extreme—higher high tides and lower low tides—and feature faster current. Seatrout can be caught on any moon phase; the full and new moons bringing "plus" high tides that often capture the attention of snook and permit fishermen are not such compelling conditions for trout anglers.

Seatrout, like other flats fish, are responsive to water level. On the rising tide, they spread out toward the crowns and interiors of the grassflats. On the falling tide, they retreat toward holes, drop-offs, and the channels surrounding the flats. The size of these fish (which runs from one to fifteen pounds) does not necessarily correlate with water depth. Trophy trout can be taken regularly in knee-deep shallow waters, while the much smaller one- to two-pound schoolies can be abundant in five to six feet of water.

Seatrout Pursuit

Many methods are effective for catching seatrout on Florida's grassflats—drifting, poling and casting, wading and casting, working the mullet muds, and chumming.

Drifting

Drifting the grassflats requires a decent vessel, such as a canoe, kayak, or flats boat, and a bit of a breeze. The prime advantage of drifting the flats for seatrout is the amount and expanse of actual fishing area that is covered, without the need for fish-spooking outboard motors. All you need to do is simply drift along. If you need to return to an upwind start area, paddle your way back in your human-powered craft. If you are in a flats boat, wait until you are well away from any fish, and then start your engine. The next step is to get back to your start area by making a wide circle track far around and away from your intended drift path.

One characteristic of drifting for seatrout involves the risk of "running over" trout with your vessel if you are fishing the upwind side and drifting suspended baits; however, there are ways of compensating for this. My tactic is to have one spinning rod drifting a mullet strip at least 120 feet away on the windward side. The long line presentation may give any "run-over" trout a chance to settle down and regroup by the time the strip bait reaches them. If I am alone, I often put this rod in the console rod holder and wrap a finger of very soft copper wire around the line to hold it in place, alongside the open bail. I always fish mullet strips for seatrout with an open bail to give them a chance to swallow the bait.

If I have another angler aboard, I arm my companion with a spinning rig sporting a standard popping cork rig and pinfish strip and suggest casting either to twelve o'clock off the bow or six o'clock off the stern, to avoid the middle drifting long line strip. I encourage popping the cork vigorously as soon as it lands and letting out a bit of line between pops. We continue this process, and as the boat drifts, the cork comes alongside the long line strip for a minute or two; then we bring in the popping cork bait and recast it off the bow or the stern again. All this is designed to cover new water on the trout flats.

Meanwhile, I always fish the downwind side of the drifting vessel into perpetually new water with a ten-pound plug rod and an appropriately effective artificial lure. As I cast downwind, the speed of my retrieve is designed to keep the line tight to get hookups on trout strikes and be in synch with the speed of the vessel as it heads toward my retrieved lure.

Poling and Casting

Poling and casting is a generic method that includes any subtle boat propulsion—such as by poles, oars, paddles, and even electric motors—toward any directed and deliberate targets on the grassflats that the angler suspects hold seatrout. In contrast to the whims of the wind in drifting, the poling and casting method is angler-controlled and determined.

Unlike specifically sighted fish, like bonefish or permit, spotted seatrout are generally not cast to as individual specimens. Rather, the poling and casting method is oriented more toward a target area. Likely areas for poling and casting include the aforementioned potholes, mini-cuts, bait schools, grass clumps, drop-offs, and mullet muds; the latter are discussed more fully later in this chapter. Experience shows that focused casting is generally more productive than blind-casting. Focused casting is even more effective when you "fan cast" a spot, such as covering a pothole with incremental clockwise casts that cover roughly 180 degrees.

With this type of fishing, artificial lures—including flies—are employed as a general practice rather than a mandate. It is possible to cast live or dead baits at specific targets, but it seems the more general preference to baitfish on the drift and anchor up when the action picks up. The repeated casting of this method generally would be too rough on live or dead baits.

The actual tactics of lure and fly fishing for spotted seatrout are similar whether you are poling and casting or wading and casting. The three criteria that should shape your casting are focusing on covering new and unspooked waters, covering the entire water column, and giving priority to seatrout ambush lairs such as potholes.

Always choose your lures and flies with matching the hatch and focal water column coverage as criteria. For instance, flies should look convincing and enticing. My favorite fly looks exactly like a darting glass minnow that I retrieve in short strips. I control the sink rate by switching from a floating line to a sink tip line. Another way to control sink rate is with the addition (or subtraction) of weighted eyes on the fly.

When you use plugs or bucktails you can determine the depth of the actual moving lure by weight, construction (like a lipped plug), and the type of retrieve you employ—your speed and rod action.

I let conditions dictate which artificial lures I use. In bright, hot, calm, midday conditions, I probe-cast along the grassflats bottom in my quest for seatrout. In cloudy conditions that feature a breeze at dawn or dusk—particularly if there are bait schools on top—I opt for surface or midsurface swimming plugs. In those conditions, I prefer to use a Devil's Horse on the surface and a YoZuri Crystal Minnow for slightly deeper operations. At all times, whatever the conditions, repeat the mantra "cover the water column" until you get trout action. If you are fishing with a companion, the two of you should work different depths with different lures or flies, utilizing different retrieves. Your portal to seatrout success is new water, different lures, and varying the retrieve.

Wading and Casting

Wading and casting lures and flies is possibly one of the most exciting and enjoyable methods of pursuing seatrout. Wading lowers your fish-spooking profile in the shallows and gives you stealth. Keep the quiet-hunter spirit alive by wading slowly and carefully.

Be careful about dragging a stringer of live seatrout too close behind you as you wade. I have lost trout to sharks more than a few times; now I leave a good distance of stringer line between myself and my trout. In addition, I keep them as close to the surface as possible with a large orange plastic float.

In the shallows, seatrout and all other flats fish are more vulnerable to weather systems aloft. You are too—exponentially so with your several feet of elevation and a potentially dangerous seven- to nine-foot lightning attractor otherwise known as a fishing rod. Pay attention to rapidly building thunderheads, blackening cloud bellies, or forming squall lines. All flats fish do to leave a flat is start flicking their tails, but you don't have that option. Unless you have a nearby flats skiff to jump into, fire up, and speed away, you will be in for a slow, tedious foot-powered retreat in the face of rapidly approaching storms. If you are wading, do not get into a foot race with oncoming weather—wait too long, and you will always lose!

Additionally, for safety's sake, make a mental note of the tidal stage and moon phase before you begin your wading for seatrout or any other flats fish. A potentially dangerous situation is to start your wading on a low spring tide level of knee-deep water, only to find that your exit or return route is hazardous or impossible six hours later due to neck deep water.

After considering all these factors, go and enjoy the adventure of a shallow water safari for a trophy-sized, orange-mouthed gator of a seatrout.

Flats Tip: Seatrout Strategy

When you are drifting the grassflats for seatrout, cover as much new water as you can. When the trout strikes begin with concentrated regularity, toss a small yet visible marker buoy overboard, so that you can return to the hot spot. As an alternative, you can drop anchor amid the strikes, but remember you must work your baits to reproduce the automatic bait momentum of drifting. As you drift along, keep an eye out for mullet muds and minnow schools—plan on thoroughly covering these potential hot spots with natural or artificial baits.

Working the Mullet Muds

Certain grassflats around Florida tend to hold more mullet muds than others. I have had excellent success fishing huge mullet muds in Biscayne Bay and Florida Bay. Think of mullet muds as naturally occurring buffet tables. Game fish like cobia and permit often follow stingrays to grab up the live food dislodged by the ray's bottom feeding. In parallel fashion, seatrout take advantage of the bottom-feeding activities of mullet schools. Anglers call these mullet muds because of the sediment stirred up into the water column—this becomes a visible seatrout clue for flats hunters. Seatrout are drawn to mullet muds for two reasons. First, the larger mullet feeding on the bottom algae stir up shrimp and small fish that the trout happily gobble up. Second, the smaller mullet within the mud often become seatrout food themselves.

Mullet muds generally occur on the wide expanses of grassflats. They remain out of reach for wading anglers; therefore, more often than not, mullet muds are a vessel-based fishery. Flats boats are the optimal vessels for this flats fishing specialty because the hottest action in a mud occurs in the freshest section, so you must have the optimal positioning to sight these new upwellings. Kayaks and canoes simply cannot provide the elevation or climbing stability that a towered flats boat offers. From your excellent vantage point atop the poling tower, it will be easier to see the freshest muds: simply pole over to the area and fish it. I have found that sighting a fresh mud and positioning yourself to fish it is best done with the use of polarized, glare-blocking glasses and a wide-brimmed hat.

In my experience natural baits have a strong advantage over artificials in the denser parts of the mud. The scent of dead bait and the scent plus vibrations of live bait are easier for seatrout to detect. An artificial lure or fly has a hard time competing with all the live food among which the seatrout are swimming.

My favorite natural baits in these conditions are live pigfish, live pinfish, live finger mullet, whitebait slabs, pinfish strips, pinfish steaks, and mullet strips. If you are intent on using artificial lures in mullet muds, make sure you use brightly colored high-contrast offerings. If you cannot draw strikes from the denser muds, work the less opaque and less turbid areas of the muds to increase your lure's visibility.

Chumming

Although chumming is not a common method of fishing for seatrout in the shallows, I have caught countless seatrout in the grassflats this way. On some of my best days, I have released over eighty trout. I particularly like this method during the windy, cloudy days of fall and spring. These conditions often make the more aesthetic and challenging methods of stalking and fishing for seatrout more difficult and prompted me to begin experimenting with chum during foul weather. Even sunny Florida can have some off days.

All you need are a decent boat, an anchor with a line, a chum bag, and a couple of frozen chum blocks in the ice chest awaiting deployment. As discussed in chapter 9, chumming for sharks on the flats evolved into a highly specialized drift method that can produce an excited and easily sighted shark rushing toward the boat. In contrast, chumming for trout is more effective on the anchor, because drifting and chumming would necessitate that the trout chase the boat—something they will not do.

Anchoring and chumming for seatrout is effective because it sends out a constant stream of scent and fish pieces. This makes the fish congregate in the chum path. Positioning your anchored boat properly is crucial. Try to get your skiff upwind and uptide of your target area to obtain a fishable and constant condition. On an incoming tide, try to position yourself in front of flats with potholes at least three feet deep. On the falling tide, get uptide of flats drop-offs. The next step is to drop a chum block into your chum bag and tie it onto one of your stern cleats. Then ease the loaded chum bag overboard.

This process takes time, just as it would if you were fishing the open expanse shallows for mackerel. As the chum melts and goes through the bag mesh in a downtide direction, things should start to happen. The first thing you should notice are the large clusters of pinfish and pilchards gathering right off your stern. You have created a "double-chum" situation for the seatrout. Although the baitfish may eat the chum particles, the scent still proceeds downtide and gets the attention of the trout. As they swim toward the source of the now strengthening scent, they encounter the pinfish and pilchard clusters. This makes them very hungry!

I have found it unproductive to cast into the baitfish balls directly astern because my presentations are inevitably attacked by the larger pinfish, blue runners, or barracuda. I have obtained my best results by casting well astern of the baitfish into the path of approaching sea-trout. I begin with two terminal rigs. One is a six-inch mullet strip fished on a 1/0 hook. The other is a small plastic-tailed jig tipped with a small piece of diced live shrimp. With this latter rig, I am always careful to tip the jig so that it will not spin on the retrieve. When these rigs stop catching fish, I start experimenting with other offerings.

Chumming the grassflats for seatrout on foul weather days can turn challenging conditions into an enjoyable, productive fishery.

Seatrout Tackle, Rigs, and Lures

The newer microbraid lines are an ideal line choice when fishing for snook or redfish tight to cover. These no-stretch lines have the sensitivity and strength to strike the fish and keep the battler out of mangroves and oyster bars. However, with spotted seatrout, this is not only unnecessary—it is contraindicated. Monofilament is a wiser choice because the slight stretch of this line is ideal for coping with the notoriously soft mouth tissues of spotsides.

Compared to the no-nonsense character of microbraid lines, monofilament puts pressure on seatrout more gingerly and delicately. Hooked seatrout often rise to the surface and thrash their heads vigorously. In these moments of battle, I have found that the no-stretch microbraid lines can slingshot lures and hooks back at the angler.

Monofilament absorbs the headshakes with less flinging of hooks and lures.

I never use a leader for seatrout. At the most, I double my line for about a foot, especially if large mangrove snapper are grabbing my baits or bucktails. Because my running line is tied directly to my hook, I prefer my line color to be clear. This is another good reason to choose monofilament for seatrout. In addition, stop-and-go lure retrieves with microbraid line require occasional hand-tightening on the reel spool that mono does not require.

It is not necessary to exceed eight-pound test line on spin and plug tackle. Eight-weight fly lines with a sink tip seem to be a prudent choice and are capable of handling even a trophy gator trout.

Most anglers currently choose graphite rod material, but I have moved in a different direction. I choose springy S-glass for my spinning and plug rods. Although this material forces me to jerk my popping plugs harder, I have found that the combination of a soft fiberglass rod and monofilament line keeps far more seatrout well hooked than do graphite rods and microbraid lines. With fly tackle, I stick with graphite rod material. I try to use a rod that loads and powers an eight-weight line optimally but also has some spring to its action.

Regarding the use of natural baits and lures, I use the finest saltwater hooks of the smallest diameter wire possible. Thin-wired saltwater hooks not only sink well, but they tend to avoid wearing a "buttonhole" slit in a trout's mouth the way thick-wired hooks do. Large buttonhole slits cause hook slips and pulls.

The popping cork is unquestionably the most popular method for seatrout on Florida's flats. The "cork" is actually a Styrofoam chugger-shaped float with a through-line passage affixed and set with a plastic dowel pin. Although the usual practice is to fish with natural baits under a popping cork, many anglers have excellent success fishing bucktails and soft plastic baits. All the angler does is pull the rod sharply, and the cup-faced end of the cork gives off a gurgling pop that seatrout seem to love. Seatrout strike at popping cork baits at any time, yet the major criterion for hookups is to wait for the cork to go down under the surface before striking. A downed cork signals that the fish has taken the bait below with its full weight and has turned away, providing a good time for an optimal hookset in the hinges of a jaw. A quick snap of the angler's wrist provides more than enough power to load the rod and line for a good hookset.

Artificial lures for seatrout are so numerous that an entire book could be written about them. The basic rule for lure selection is to keep a wide variety of lures available to cover every possible situation for seatrout on the flats. The features that guide what you keep in your tackle box should include shape, texture, color, action, weight, and operating depth.

Finally, always have a landing net available when seatrout fishing on the flats. A landing net is essential if you want to keep a seatrout or two for the table—this applies when wading and triply so when fishing from a flats boat. In the latter case, swinging a seatrout aboard your boat almost guarantees a hook pullout because the fish's delicate mouth tissue now has to bear its entire dead weight. If the fish is to be released, a net is important in minimizing the hook hole in the trout's mouth.

Flats Hot Spots: Seatrout in Biscayne Bay

Two places offer great success for seatrout in Florida's grassflats, and both of them are conveniently situated in Biscayne Bay right off Miami. One area lies in North Biscayne Bay, just north of the Julia Tuttle Causeway: you can fish the huge grassflat behind Mount Sinai Hospital on the east side of the bay, or alternatively, fish the grassflat east of the Palm Bay Tower on 67th Street on the west side of the bay. In South Biscayne Bay, you can find good seatrout fishing south of Rickenbacker Causeway right off the Vizcaya Estate on the mainland side.

14

The Future of Wild Florida's Flats

A good model for getting a past, present, and future-based understanding of Florida's flats—and their fishing   is to view matters from two standpoints: those of planetary movements and human movements.

Planetary Movements

Planetary movements are the physical events that are naturally occurring phenomena of the Earth. They are not caused by humans but certainly affect us. Planetary movements can be massive and irregular and can cause irreversible changes—a climate change can bring an end to an entire range of life forms.

Seasonal and regular planetary movements are naturally occurring phenomena too, but they are events from which the possible changes and damage are not irreversible. Seasonal planetary movements exist because of the geophysical workings of Earth and its place in the solar system.

The events that are provoked over, adjacent to, or on Florida's flats by seasonal planetary movements include hurricanes, tornadoes, thunderstorms, lightning-based fires, and cold fronts. These events are parts of the life of a Florida flats angler. They are understandable, and some people theorize that they have a purpose—they are momentarily chaotic but part of a much larger planetary order. Hurricanes, for instance, serve to transfer heat and energy between the equator and the poles.

Thunderstorms over Florida's vast wilderness can create numerous air-to-ground lightning strikes. If the ground below is dry, it can spark, tinder, and spring into a large-scale fire that sweeps across the area for miles. Yet eventually, out from under the burnt ground and ash, new plant forms spring up through an enriched soil. These events have occurred from time immemorial and are part of a rhythm and order behind the surface chaos.

In recent years more than ever, we earthlings, including Floridians, have learned that planetary events can affect us dramatically but are entirely outside human control. Planetary plates shift, hurricanes spin, rivers flood, and surface life forms can be impacted in colossal ways. Periodically, Florida's Everglades goes ablaze after a molten kiss from a storm's lightning bolt. Nature does not consider humankind, yet humankind must consider nature. It was this way in the past, and it will be this way in the future.

Human Movements

It does not demand a keen eye to realize that people's movements and the effects of human activity pose the greatest threat, not just to the future of Florida's flats but to Earth as a whole. All you need to do is be aware and observe!

Indeed, out toward the coastline along the marshes and mangroves, the sea life turns round and round in a cycle that, left alone, has its own unique type of order. There is a saying that to know where you are going, you need to know where you have been; and with human movement as it impacts wild Florida's flats, the trend has gone from teeming abundance toward a habitat that may be vanishing into history.

In my efforts to ponder the future of Florida's flats by plunging into its past, I turned to Captain Bill Curtis. For me, talking with him is an encounter with living, breathing Florida flats history. He took me back fifty years and told me tales of Old Florida's flats. I was struck by his images of abundant fish stocks and habitats where nonstop flats action unfolded all day long only minutes from a boat-launching ramp.

He talked and I listened.

As he talked on, I detected the growth of a dark force against nature in Florida—unaware, unbalanced, and unchecked human activity. It became clear to me that the early flats anglers of Florida were cautious and respectful of the environment. They had a tradition of reverence for "nonimpact" on Florida's flats that unfortunately did not extend to other people and later activities. As Florida grew and people came, cities and factories mushroomed and created new forms of pollution for Florida's wilderness. The soil and the underground aquifer became soaked with industrial chemicals. Sewers and storm drainage belched poisons into our rivers, grasslands, marshes, beaches, and bays. Vaporous chemicals belched skyward—nibbling away at our planet's protective sheath and causing a warming of our waters that goes unchecked as this is written.

As the multitudes thronged to Florida, people needed living arrangements. In response to this need, building proceeded feverishly along our coastline. Land grew scarcer, and housing went vertical along our bays and beaches. Concrete structures rose up that would brazenly block out the sky and gobble up vertical habitat. This trend continues in the present with ferocity of replication and spread—some people call this progress, but for natural Florida, it is a cancer.

Government responded to commercial demands and channelized the southern half of Florida. This choked off the precious sheetflow of water to the Everglades and Florida Bay. Commercial overfishing decimated shrimp stocks, crabs, and other bottom life-forms that were necessary to our water world—they also formed the food source for the flats fish of Florida. Fish like mutton snapper became scarce on the flats because they were overfished on the reefs offshore. Through Bill's tales I came to understand what all of today's Florida flats anglers must understand: that our world and the fish that live in it are a mere fragment of their prior numbers and greatness.

The recreational pleasures of new Floridians taking to the water created new demands for excitement. Industry responded to this demand and created powered vessels—designed purely for speed and sensation—that are capable of roaring over flats in mere inches of water. Often, the people who use them are wrapped up in their excited pleasures, unaware that their activity is a 747 over the life-forms mere inches below.

An hour later, Bill Curtis's talk brought us to the present, and it was clear that a challenge lies at the feet of people who live in Florida or visit. Humanity, not nature, creates the cloud that hovers over wild Florida's flats: what the future will be in its shadow is entirely up to you and me.

About the Art

Vaughn Cochran

I don't consider myself a marine artist; I'm really a contemporary painter who happens to paint fish.

The world of sporting art and especially fishing art is filled with many great artists who over the years have painted every fish in every possible pose. Where do you go from there? How do you make an artistic statement that anybody even cares about, much less one that satisfies yourself?

Most of the painting being done today is illustration work, rendering the fish more or less as it appears in nature, with the background being the only part of the painting that displays any creativity by the artist. So how do you say something different about fish? What can you do to paint a landscape or seascape in a new light, so to speak? If you try to answer those questions with your paintbrush, you are approaching the definition of a contemporary painter who happens to paint fish.

I've chosen a couple of different approaches for my art, one being the use of color and another being to use composition as a tool to present a common scene or event in an unusual or unexpected way.

I hope that over the years my work will be viewed just as good art, on the same basis that other contemporary art is judged—not necessarily for the subject matter but for handling of paint, overall design, color, and all the design elements that make up the art itself.

Reproductions available
Vaughn Cochran Studio
904-692-4419
www.vaughncochranart.com

Contributors

Rene Austin

Contact Rene Austin at
Ranger Boats
Flippin, Arkansas 72634
Telephone: 870-453-2222 or 870-453-2201, ext. 2203
Fax: 870-453-2306
E-mail: rene.austin@rangerboats.com
Web site: www.rangerboats.com

Tim Borski

Tim Borski paints unique wildlife art in watercolor, oils, and acrylics, and can be found daily in his studio in Islamorada in the Florida Keys. He has painted seriously since his college days in central Wisconsin, where he was born and raised. In a style all his own, he focuses primarily on bird and fish species and waxes eloquent about their attributes and habitats. His paintings are often given as prizes in Keys fishing tournaments, and his artwork can be found worldwide, thanks in part to the exposure these tournaments have given him. His artwork has graced T-shirts, business cards, restaurant promotional material, and most recently a line of Patagonia clothing.

Sometimes Tim escapes the easel to go fishing in the backcountry of the Keys, gathering inspiration and photographs for his art. He loves fishing of all kinds and enjoys the chase as much as if not more than the catch. He likes to experiment with different flies, lures, and methods and is rarely bored while fishing. He has traveled in pursuit of his avocation and has enjoyed opportunities to fish nationwide and in Canada, Panama, Costa Rica, Guatemala, England, Scotland, the ABC Islands, the Bahamas, and more.

Another reason to be out on the water is for filming. Tim and Captain Jon Milchman, also of Islamorada, produced two Borski Ties Flies videos in 2004. Each DVD features Tim showing how to tie five unique flies, and then using the flies in real fishing situations for various species. The beauty of the backcountry, the sport, and the fish are highlighted, and all fish are released.

A recent endeavor is working with a boat manufacturer, East Cape Canoes, to create a "T. Borski" line of specialized small skiffs and canoes. Tim's artwork is displayed in the form of wraps on these vessels.

Tim writes, too, and his work has been published in several magazines. He writes a quarterly how-to column on flies for the *Redbone Journal,* and has a dozen trademarked fly patterns to his credit through the Umpqua Feather Merchants. Often his articles are highlighted by his own artistic illustrations.

Borski illustrated Flip Pallot's book *Memories, Mangroves and Magic* and twice appeared on Pallot's ESPN fishing show, *Walker's Cay Chronicles.* He appeared on Rick Murphy's *Sportsman's Adventures* in a shark fishing episode and in two 2006 episodes of the ESPN cable show *Guide House Montauk,* showcasing fishing captains in Montauk, New York. Tim appears aboard a fishing boat during a charity tournament and in the guide's house tying flies. While Tim enjoys traveling, he could not live anywhere else in the world unless the fishing was as interesting and challenging as it is in the Florida Keys. He established roots in the Keys more than twenty years ago and they are not likely to be unearthed, hurricanes notwithstanding. He and his wife, Jill, a writer, have two young sons, Josef and Gus, who are following in their father's footsteps with a love of nature and their own fascination with sea creatures and waterspouts.

Contact Tim Borski at
Telephone/Fax: 305-852-9886

E-mail: tborski@earthlink.net
Web site: www.borskiflies.com

Vaughn Cochran

Vaughn Cochran is an artist, fly fisherman, and conservationist. He says he has always been an artist, even when not making his living at it; he's always been a fisherman, though not always a fly fisherman; and he's always been a conservationist, except when he didn't know any better.

A native Floridian, Vaughn grew up in the art community of St. Augustine and earned art degrees in ceramics and painting at the University of South Florida. Arriving in Key West in 1972, he started his fishing career and also became an original member of Jimmy Buffett's Coral Reefer Band. That was a great time to be in Key West, he says.

Vaughn became one of the most respected fly fishing guides in the Florida Keys and found plenty of artistic inspiration observing nature while guiding his clients to meet the challenges of saltwater fly fishing. For several years he fished and painted in Mexico's Yucatan Peninsula, and he later managed the famous fishing lodge Parismina Tarpon Rancho in Costa Rica. Now retired from guiding, he recently spent a year as fishing manager at Belize's classic Turneffe Island Lodge.

Vaughn's artwork has been shown in numerous galleries and exhibitions in the United States and has received many awards. His paintings and sculptures are held in private and corporate collections. Recently his work was featured in a one-man show at the International Game Fish Association Fishing Hall of Fame and Museum main gallery. Although he still paints the traditional fishing scenes and seascapes for which he is known, some of his newest work revisits the pop-art fish with which he started his career.

These paintings are now available as prints, as are many of his more traditional scenes of the flats he fished on a regular basis. Vaughn's powerful and popular sumi-style Black Fly logo merchandise includes T-shirts, license tags, mugs, hats, note cards, and boat decals. Black Fly merchandise and other Vaughn Cochran T-shirts and products are available at www.vaughncochranart.com, through catalogs, and in specialty fly shops throughout the United States. His love of fishing has also landed him the opportunity to be the featured co-host and guide for several episodes of ESPN's morning lineup of fishing shows, including *Fly Fishing America, Fly Fishing the World, North American Fisherman, Back Roads* with Ron Shara, and *Spanish Fly* with José Wejebe in Belize.

Contact Vaughn Cochran at

Telephone: Vaughn Cochran Studio 904-692-4419; Black Fly Outfitter 904-826-0000

Web site: www.vaughncochranart.com

Captain Butch Constable

Butch grew up in Palm Beach and learned to fish all the marine waters from Palm Beach to Stuart, Florida. As a teenager he developed a love for diving and examining reef fish in the early 1970s. A few years later, Butch's family moved to Green Turtle Cay, Abaco, where Butch added bonefishing as a learned specialty. After that he shifted his explorations to the Florida Keys, where he specialized in flats fishing for tarpon.

His base of operations is in Jupiter, Florida, where he has plied the waters for more than thirty-five years. Butch Constable comes as close as any guide to being a snook fishing legend along the Treasure Coast and Gold Coast. He is well known for developing the craft and techniques of live chumming for snook along East Coast Florida beaches and inside flats. He has been the driving force behind the development of plumbed and pumped livewell systems in flats and bay boats. His records indicate that he has caught and released more than 120,000 snook over his long career.

Butch is equally adept at offshore fishing for all the popular game fish and has a twenty-five-foot vessel and a nineteen-foot flats skiff. His is a familiar face at many Florida fishing seminars and shows.

Contact Captain Butch Constable at

Telephone: 561-747-6665

Cell phone: 561-758-6267

Captain Jon Cooper

Jon can best be described as a fishing guide who really loves fishing: all the rest follows. Although he concentrates as an expert on the flats of Biscayne Bay, where he has been guiding since 1992, he is equally at home and proficient from the Gold Coast back bays out to the Gulf Stream. Jon's love of the sea means there is no purist egotism here: everyone is welcome. He can take you out with the rising sun to catch beautiful spotted seatrout and tasty snappers or for a sandflat triumph, catching a bonefish, tarpon, or permit. If your dream is to battle high-flying sailfish and speedy bonito out in the ocean, or the toothy barracuda, or even the backbreaking shark, he'll zip you right out there. He is a total guide.

Jon's background is diverse. He was born in India. His British parents brought him to the United States in 1968 and raised him on Florida's beautiful West Coast, where his love for the sea emerged. He has had a successful career as an engineer, topping out in his profession. That success is reflected in his proclivities and his striving for precision and excellence.

Jon is a funny and intelligent person whose quest for diversion and adventure permeates every fishing trip. Fishing with him may mean bright highlights of battling and releasing a fast-running permit or silvery, jumping tarpon, yet above all, Jon provides memories of fun, adventure, and love of the sea.

Contact Captain Jon Cooper at
Telephone: 954-584-0250
E-mail: coop@captaincooper.com
Web site: www.captaincooper.com

Captain Bill Curtis

Bill Curtis comes as close as anyone to being a living legend in the world of Florida light tackle and flats fishing—his experience, expertise, and knowledge are sufficient to fill ten books.

Bill was born in Oklahoma but has spent most of his life in South Florida and the Florida Keys. He began fishing in Biscayne Bay in 1948 and began guiding those waters in 1958 out of Key Biscayne for bonefish, tarpon, and permit.

He is the first guide to have offered poled flats fishing trips across vast Biscayne Bay. His flats fishing has led him across the Caribbean, but his life as expert guide has been in Florida waters from Miami to Key West to Homosassa.

Bill has been featured in many television shows, and countless articles have been written about him. His current passion for and devotion to Florida flats fishing has involved him with Bonefish and Tarpon Unlimited, of which he is a founder. This organization is devoted to research and interventions designed to understand, preserve, and restore bonefish and tarpon stocks for the present and the future. He has been responsible for launching the careers of many flats guides. Bill Curtis is one of the originators of flats fishing, a marine fishing specialty that began in Florida and has grown worldwide in its popularity.

Contact Captain Bill Curtis at
Telephone: 305-279-6699

Pat Ford

Pat Ford was born and raised in northern New Jersey, fishing in most every body of water that was available to him. He entered the University of Notre Dame in 1961, where as a communications arts major, he added sports photography to his passions. After graduating in 1965, he entered Columbia Law School in New York City. After being admitted to the New York Bar in 1968, he joined the Navy JAG Corps and was stationed in Pensacola where he began writing for *Salt Water Sportsman* magazine and several others. When he was transferred from Pensacola to Key West, it became very clear that he was going to spend the rest of his life in Florida. After discharge from the Navy in December 1972 he moved to Miami and began his law practice, specializing in civil litigation. He has been board certified in civil trial law since 1983. For over 35 years now, Pat has continued to fish, take photos, and write about his experiences on the water. He has traveled extensively and has held over a dozen IGFA Fly Rod World Records ranging from a 196 lb tiger shark caught in Florida Bay to a 14.5 lb tigerfish caught in Zambia, Africa. His first book on his fishing travels, *The Best Fly Fishing Trips Money Can Buy* (2006), is designed to help anglers duplicate the best fishing vacations that he has experienced. Pat is currently working on *A Passion for Tarpon* with Andy Mill for Wild River Press. His extensive photo collection can be seen at patfordphotos.com

Contact Pat Ford at
Telephone: 305-670-2000
Fax: 305-670-1353
E-mail: tpfordjr@bellsouth.net
Web site: www.patfordphotos.com

Scott S. Heywood

Scott began his angling career fly fishing the small streams of northern Michigan. His goal as a young man was to become well versed in such wilderness skills as mountaineering and rock climbing, whitewater rafting, sea kayaking, skiing, and hunting. In each of these exciting endeavors, he was sure to take a fly rod with him. Kayaking exotic environs like Idaho's Salmon River, he'd catch trout. His kayaking sojourns in the Bahamas, Alaska, and Russia provided the waters for Scott to catch bonefish, salmon, and taimen. His foundation as explorer, adventurous athlete, and angler was based on his true love of wild places.

After many years of owning and operating an outdoor equipment store in Sheridan, Wyoming, in 1991 he started a fly fishing travel company called Angling Destinations. He did not begin this as a travel agent: to the contrary, he evolved into his role as travel consultant because angler after angler began calling Angling Destinations to ask questions about fishing in the remote destinations Scott and his associates were actively exploring. They used the knowledge they had gained about the world's wild places to help dedicated anglers plan productive and rewarding angling adventures.

Today, Angling Destinations has established itself as one of the leaders in the field of fly fishing and light tackle fishing travel companies, specializing in flats, shallow water, and sight fishing. Scott's company

offers trips to exotic and unpressured destinations the world over, and he continues to search for new and pristine angling locations.
Contact Scott S. Heywood at
Telephone: 800-211-8530
E-mail: scott@anglingdestinations.com
Web site: www.anglingdestinations.com

Captain John Kumiski

Writer, author, speaker, teacher, fishing guide, fly tyer, husband, and father, John Kumiski has fished in fourteen states and ten countries and has logged thousands of days fishing Florida waters, concentrating most of his efforts along the Space Coast.

A member of the Florida Outdoor Writers Association and the Southeastern Outdoor Press Association, John has written eight books and parts of several others, has penned hundreds of magazine articles, and has had thousands of images published. He has spoken at fishing shows and to fishing and other clubs all over the United States. His willingness to share his expertise, his stunning photography, and his sense of humor result in frequent repeat performances at many clubs and shows.

Brevard Community College calls upon John to teach fishing classes several times a year. A Federation of Fly Fishers certified fly casting instructor, he teaches both conventional flats fishing and saltwater fly fishing classes.

John has been guiding fishermen in Space Coast waters since 1987. While specializing in fly fishing, he also caters to conventional tackle anglers. Redfish are the most common fish, but tarpon, snook, seatrout, black drum, cobia, tripletail, and more may make up the day's catch. His files are full of photos and letters from happy anglers who have made outstanding catches with his help.

Several books and magazine articles have featured John's fly tying skills. Some of his original patterns include the Fuzzy Crab, Son of Clouser, Konehead, Mosquito Lagoon Special, and the SexyFly series.

Susan Kumiski has remained a steady fixture in John's life for more than twenty-five years. They and their sons Maxx and Alex share their home with two cats, several bicycles, nine boats, and lots and lots of books. No one is quite sure how many fishing rods live there.

Contact Captain John Kumiski at

Telephone: 407-977-5207

E-mail: john@spottedtail.com

Web site: www.spottedtail.com

Captain Mike Locklear

Mike was born to fish in Homosassa, Florida. As a young boy, he fished at the side of his dad, a famous fishing guide and one of the pioneers of the Homosassa tarpon fishery from the 1950s to the 1970s. The two shared many fond fishing trips along the Homosassa River. Mike fell in love with Gulf fishing when his grandfather, also a guide, took him on his first boat trip for seatrout. In 1971, his dad took him to the then famous tarpon flats, where acre-sized schools of tarpon roamed. At age fifteen Mike landed his first tarpon, a giant of 184 pounds, using a Harold LeMaster Mirrolure.

After graduating from Crystal River High School, Mike began his career as a guide for a private fishing club in 1976, where he put his first client on a large river-caught tarpon. That same year he became a member of the Homosassa Guides Association, which is still going strong today.

From 1977 to 1982 Mike captained various yachts on both coasts of Florida and in the Bahamas, catching game fish from dolphin to blue marlin while enjoying weekly summer scuba diving trips to Cay Sal Banks for lobster, grouper, snapper, and conch.

During the mid-eighties Mike returned to his home waters, where he began building his local guiding career with the help of many people in the fishing industry and the media. This was the beginning of more than five thousand charter days on the water in twenty years.

Mike devoted himself to lobbying Governor Martinez in 1989 for the historic no-sale status of redfish. From 1990 onward, his new passion became fly fishing for tarpon in the spring months, during which hosts of world-class anglers have enjoyed many good battles with the silver king.

Mike has been active with the Coastal Conservation Association of Florida for more than twenty years and is also involved with Tarpon and Bonefish Unlimited, in which he has served as a chapter president.

A hundred or more successful fishing trips with writers and TV producers have portrayed this congenial and professional guide to the public's eye. Happily married for twenty years with two beautiful children, Mike remains at the top of his game, guiding from a highly technical and very shallow draft Hell's Bay Marquesa poling skiff.

Contact Captain Mike Locklear at
Telephone: 352-628-4207
Cell phone: 352-422-1927
E-mail: captmike@homosassafishing.com
Web site: www.homosassafishing.com

Captain Greg Poland

Greg is a native of South Florida. He left the FBI to pursue a career as a fishing guide for flats fishing in the beautiful waters of the Florida Keys and the backcountry of the Everglades National Park. He lives in the upper central Keys in Islamorada but trailers or runs his boats to where the flats action occurs on any given day.

His training and experience have given him highly diverse abilities. He holds a master's license through the U.S. Coast Guard and he is equally at home at the helm of a huge sport fishing yacht or in a small shallow water skiff. Captain Greg teaches fly fishing at a school in the Florida Keys, and he has helped in the design of two popular flats fishing skiffs.

Captain Greg has guided anglers to championships in some of the most prestigious flats fishing tournaments in the world. He has guided his anglers to catching and attaining world record status for tarpon, bonefish, and other species. It is likely that you have seen him on numerous television fishing shows, where he is highly sought after by producers as a friendly and expert guest.

Contact Captain Greg Poland at
Telephone: 305-852-9940
E-mail: gregpoland@mac.com
Web site: www.gregpoland.com

Captain Tom Rowland

Tom grew up in Chattanooga, Tennessee. He fished this area with his father, and those times spent together were the foundation of Tom's passion for angling. While working in Yellowstone National Park, Tom backpacked and fished the better part of this fishing paradise. He then began his guiding career in Jackson Hole, Wyoming, on the finest western trout rivers.

In 1994 Tom became a U.S. Coast Guard-licensed captain. After a year of training and exploring the waters of the Florida Keys and the backcountry of the Everglades National Park, Captain Rowland began guiding out of Key West. His competitive pursuits have forced him to learn all areas westward from Key West to Port Aransas, Texas, and up the East Coast to South Carolina.

Today, he operates Big Blue Fishing, Inc., which features charter vessels and guides for flats, inshore, and offshore fishing. Captain Tom is distinctive in developing the use of a twenty-four-foot bay boat as a vessel for flats and offshore fishing on the same charter. He also operates a very shallow draft technical poling skiff.

Tom Rowland is a prominent presence at national fishing shows, casting competitions, and professional tournaments as well as on television and radio shows. He is known for his combination of perfectionism, drive, and patience, while remaining extremely approachable. These qualities make it obvious why both novice and expert have sought him as their guide in world-renowned tournament championships. Anglers from around the world may know Tom better through his television series *Inshore Xtremes*.

Contact Captain Tom Rowland at
Telephone/Fax: 305-294-7447
Cell phone: 305-797-2238
E-mail: tom@saltwaterexperience.com
Web site: www.saltwaterexperience.com

Captain Robert "RT" Trosset

Captain "RT" is one of the premier light tackle and fly fishing guides in the Florida Keys and has been for over thirty years. His expertise covers all of the flats, middle, and offshore waters of the entire area from Key Largo to the Dry Tortugas and beyond. His charter vessels are a thirty-four-foot Yellowfin and an eighteen-foot Hell's Bay Marquesa, both powered by Suzuki Outboards.

In 2004, the International Game Fish Association honored him for becoming the first captain to lead clients to one hundred world records. The current total stands at 160. His oldest son, Robert Trosset III, is taking over the family business. Give him a call to book a charter.
Contact Captain Robert "RT" Trosset at
Telephone: 305-294-5801

About the Author

Jan Stephen Maizler specializes in writing about human potential and saltwater angling. He has published more than two hundred magazine and Web site articles and eight books. His most recent books are *Flats Fishing II: A Shoalwater Handbook, Fishing Florida's Coast, The Transformation Handbook*, and *The Relationship Handbook*. Jan has been fishing in salt water since 1952 and began specializing in flats fishing in 1962. He is a former International Game Fish Association world record holder for bonefish (8 pounds, 4 ounces, on two-pound line) and permit (23 pounds, 15 ounces, on four-pound line). Over his angling career, Jan has caught and released more than two thousand bonefish, one thousand tarpon, and four hundred permit on Florida's flats. He can be visited online at www.fishingfloridasflats.com, www.flatsfishingonline.com, www.transformationhandbook.com, and www.relationshiphandbook.com.